Pictured: Peter Larkin's 1984 Tony Award nominated scenic design set "The Rink"

The Rink

A NEW MUSICAL

Book by
Terrence McNally

Music by
John Kander

Lyrics by
Fred Ebb

No part of this book may be reproduced, stored in a retrieval system, or transmitted in any form, by any means, including mechanical, electronic, photocopying, recording, or otherwise, without the prior written permission of the publisher.

SAMUEL FRENCH, INC.
45 WEST 25TH STREET   NEW YORK 10010
7623 SUNSET BOULEVARD   HOLLYWOOD 90046
LONDON   *TORONTO*

Book Copyright ©, 1985, by Terrence McNally.
Lyrics Copyright ©, 1983, 1985, by Fiddleback Music
Publishing Co., Inc. and Kander & Ebb, Inc., with the exception of
"The Apple Doesn't Fall"; "Quintet—Part I"; and
"We Can Make It (Reprise)," which are Copyright ©, 1984, 1985,
by Fiddleback Music Publishing Co., Inc. and Kander & Ebb, Inc.

ALL RIGHTS RESERVED

Amateurs wishing to arrange for the production of THE RINK must make application to SAMUEL FRENCH, INC., at 45 West 25th Street, New York N.Y. 10010, giving the following particulars:

(1) The name of the town and theatre or hall in which it is proposed to give the production.
(2) The maximum seating capacity of the theatre or hall.
(3) Scale of ticket prices.
(4) The number of performances it is intended to give, and the dates thereof.
(5) Indicate whether you will use an orchestration or simply a piano.

Upon receipt of these particulars SAMUEL FRENCH, INC., will quote terms and availability.

Stock royalty quoted on application to SAMUEL FRENCH, INC., 45 West 25th Street, New York, N.Y. 10010.

For all other rights than those stipulated above apply to Bridget Aschenberg, International Creative Management, Inc., 40 West 57th Street, New York, New York 10019; or to Gilbert Parker, William Morris Agency, Inc. 1350 Avenue of the Americas, New York, N.Y. 10019.

An orchestration consisting of:

Piano/Conductor's Score (Rehearsal Piano)
Reed I (Flute, Piccolo, Clarinet, Soprano & Alto Saxophones)
Reed II (Clarinet, Bass Clarinet, Alto Saxophone)
Reed III (Flute, Clarinet, Oboe, English Horn, Tenor Saxophone)
Reed IV (Flute, Clarinet, Bassoon, Baritone Saxophone)
Trumpets I & II
Trumpet III
Trombone I
Trombone II
Trombone III
Violins (4 Players, 2 Desks) (2 Books)
Celli (2 Players) (2 Books)
Guitar (Acoustic, Electric, & Banjo)
Bass (Acoustic & Electric)
Drums (also Tympani & Glockenspiel)
Keyboards (Piano, Yamaha Electric Grand Piano, Synthesizer)

will be loaned two months prior to the production ONLY on receipt of the royalty quoted for all performances, the rental fee and a refundable deposit. The deposit will be refunded on the safe return to SAMUEL FRENCH, INC. of all materials loaned for the production.

Anyone presenting the play shall not commit or authorize any act or omission by which the copyright of the play or the right to copyright same may be impaired.

No changes shall be made in the play for the purpose of your production unless authorized in writing.

The publication of this play does not imply that it is necessarily available for performance by amateurs or professionals. Amateurs and professionals considering a production are strongly advised to apply to Samuel French, Inc., for consent before starting rehearsals, advertising, or booking a theatre or hall.

Printed in U.S.A.
ISBN 0 573 68172 4

Important Advertising and Billing Requirements

ALL producers of THE RINK must give the following credit notice in all programs in the following form:

>(Name of Producer)
>presents
>THE RINK
>
>Book by TERRENCE McNALLY
>Music by JOHN KANDER
>Lyrics by FRED EBB

The names of Terrence McNally, John Kander and Fred Ebb must appear in any and all advertising, publicity, and exploitation of the play for amateur and stock production. Their names must appear in all theatre programs, houseboards, billboards, advertisements, marquees, displays, posters, throwaways, circulars, announcements, and whenever and wherever the title of the play appears immediately following the title of the play. The names of Terrence McNally, John Kander and Fred Ebb must be equal in size, type and prominence, and at least 50% of the size, type and prominence of the title type or the type accorded to the name of the play, whichever is larger. No credits shall appear in type larger or more prominent than the credit to Terrence McNally, John Kander and Fred Ebb except for the title of the play.

MARTIN BECK THEATRE
OWNED AND OPERATED BY JUJAMCYN THEATERS
RICHARD G. WOLFF, PRESIDENT

Jules Fisher   Roger Berlind
and
Joan Cullman   Milbro Productions   Kenneth-John Productions, Inc.
in association with Jonathan Farkas

present

Chita Rivera   Liza Minnelli

in

The Rink

Book by **Terrence McNally**   Music by **John Kander**   Lyrics by **Fred Ebb**

with

Jason Alexander   Ronn Carroll   Scott Ellis   Scott Holmes
Mel Johnson, Jr.   Frank Mastrocola   Kimi Parks

Scenery Designed by **Peter Larkin**   Costumes Designed by **Theoni V. Aldredge**   Lighting Designed by **Marc B. Weiss**

Sound Designed by **Otts Munderloh**   Hair and Make-up by **J. Roy Helland**

Musical Director **Paul Gemignani**   Musical Conductor and Dance Arrangements **Tom Fay**   Orchestrations by **Michael Gibson**

Assistant Choreographer **Tina Paul**   Associate Producer **Tina Chen**   Music Publisher **Tommy Valando**

General Management **Marvin A. Krauss**   Casting **Johnson-Liff Associates**   Press Representation **Merle Debuskey**

Produced in association with Jujamcyn Theaters Corp., Richard G. Wolff, President

Executive Producer
Robin Ullman

Choreography by
Graciela Daniele

Directed by
A.J. Antoon

Original Cast Album on Polydor Records and Cassettes.
Manufactured and Marketed by Poly Gram Records

The Producers and Theatre Management are Members
of The League of New York Theatres and Producers, Inc.

CAST
(in order of appearance)

Angel	LIZA MINNELLI
Little Girl	KIMI PARKS

The Wreckers:
Lino	JASON ALEXANDER
Buddy	MEL JOHNSON, JR.
Guy	SCOTT HOLMES
Lucky	SCOTT ELLIS
Tony	FRANK MASTROCOLA
Ben	RONN CARROLL

Anna	CHITA RIVERA
Dino	SCOTT HOLMES
Dino's Father	RONN CARROLL
Lenny	JASON ALEXANDER
Hiram	MEL JOHNSON, JR.
Tom	FRANK MASTROCOLA
Sugar	SCOTT ELLIS
Punk	FRANK MASTROCOLA
Punk	SCOTT ELLIS
Punk	JASON ALEXANDER
Mrs. Silverman	RONN CARROLL
Mrs. Jackson	MEL JOHNSON, JR.

(continued)

Arnie	SCOTT ELLIS
Charlie	MEL JOHNSON, JR.
Uncle Fausto	JASON ALEXANDER
Suitor	SCOTT ELLIS
Suitor	MEL JOHNSON, JR.
Suitor	FRANK MASTROCOLA
Father Rocco	SCOTT HOLMES
Bobby Perillo	SCOTT ELLIS
Sister Philomena	RONN CARROLL
Peter Reilly	FRANK MASTROCOLA
Junior Miller	MEL JOHNSON, JR.
Debbie Duberman	SCOTT HOLMES
Danny	SCOTT ELLIS

STANDBYS AND UNDERSTUDIES

Standbys and Understudies never substitute for listed players unless a specific announcement for the appearance is made at the time of the performance.

Standby for MS. RIVERA — PATTI KARR
Standby for MS. MINNELLI — MARY TESTA
Understudy for Lino, Lucky and Tony—ROB MARSHALL; for Guy—FRANK MASTROCOLA; for Ben and Buddy—JIM TUSHAR; for Little Girl—BARCLAY DeVEAU.

Place: A roller rink somewhere on the Eastern seaboard.
Time: The 1970's.

MUSICAL NUMBERS

ACT I

"Colored Lights" .... **Angel**
"Chief Cook and Bottle Washer" .... **Anna**
"Don't Ah Ma Me" .... **Anna and Angel**
"Blue Crystal" .... **Dino**
"Under the Roller Coaster" .... **Angel**
"Not Enough Magic" .... **Dino, Angel, Anna, Sugar, Hiram, Tom, Lenny and Dino's Father**
"We Can Make It" .... **Anna**
"After All These Years" .... **The Wreckers**
"Angel's Rink and Social Center" .... **Angel and The Wreckers**
"What Happened to the Old Days?" ... **Anna, Mrs. Silverman and Mrs. Jackson**
"Colored Lights" (Reprise) .... **Angel**

ACT II

"The Apple Doesn't Fall" .... **Anna and Angel**
"Marry Me" .... **Lenny**
"We Can Make It" (Reprise) .... **Anna**
"Mrs. A." .... **Anna, Angel, Lenny and Suitors**
"The Rink" .... **The Wreckers**
"Wallflower" .... **Anna and Angel**
"All the Children in a Row" .... **Angel and Danny**
Coda .... **Anna and Angel**

A NOTE

THE RINK is a small musical. Two women and six men. The women are ANNA and ANGEL. The men are THE WRECKERS. In the flashbacks, the men will play all the people in ANNA's and ANGEL's past: men and women; young and old.

THE RINK is a story of forgiveness. Mother and daughter learn to let go of the past in order to be free to move into the future.

The Rink

ACT ONE

Darkness. Silence. There is no overture.

[MUSIC CUE 1: COLORED LIGHTS]

We hear a sturdy, solid, oom-pah-pah vamp on a pipe organ. It is repeated twice.

And then we hear a rushing guitar figure. It is repeated restlessly. It alternates with the organ vamp.

A light comes up DS., *revealing a figure whose back is turned to us.*

The organ vamp is repeated. So is the guitar figure. They alternate again.

The figure onstage turns, and we see a young woman. She is 30 years old. She is attractive but somewhat overweight. Indeed, most of her physical possibilities have either been overlooked or underdeveloped. She looks like hundreds, no, thousands of young women who have not realized their own specialness because no one ever told them that they were.

Her name is ANGEL. She wears a coat, jeans, sneakers, and is carrying a suitcase. She is clearly traveling. Her eyes are fixed on that place she is going to. From the way they glow, that place is very clear to her.

We hear an announcer's voice droning over a loudspeaker system.

ANNOUNCER. (*BEN*) Trailways bus departing for Chicago and points east now boarding, platform three. Trailways bus departing for Chicago and points east now boarding, platform three.

THE RINK

ANGEL begins to sing "COLORED LIGHTS."

ANGEL.
I WAS SITTING ON A SAND DUNE IN SANTA CRUZ, OR MONTEREY
WELL, ANYWAY
I COULD FEEL THE TRICKLE ON MY CHEEK OF OCEAN SPRAY — A PERFECT DAY
WELL, ANYWAY
I REMEMBER THAT I TURNED TO SAM AND SAID . . . OR WAS IT FRED?
WELL, ANYWAY
I SHOULD BE UP AND YET, I'M DOWN INSTEAD
SOMETHING'S MISSING, SAM
SOMETHING'S MISSING, FRED
SOMETHING'S MISSING HERE

(*Through the scrim behind her the lights begin to come up on the interior of a magnificent old roller rink: the most magical, romantic place imaginable.*)

WHERE ARE MY COLORED LIGHTS?
BEADS AND BLEACHERS AND COLORED LIGHTS?
PASSING SMILES, ROUND AND ROUND
THUMPING OOM PAH PAH ORGAN SOUND
NOISY BOYS, LONG AND LEAN
GIGGLES OF GIRLS IN THE MEZZANINE
FILTERED THROUGH
COLORED LIGHTS
GOLD AND AMBER AND GREEN

I WAS SAILING OUT OF LONG BEACH ON A CATAMARAN, OR FISHING SCOW
WELL, ANYHOW
I WAS LEANING, CHEWING CASHEWS, OFF THE STARBOARD BOW, THAT SUNSET, WOW!
WELL, ANYHOW
I REMEMBER TELLING JOEY, "GOD, YOU'RE SWEET"
OR WAS IT PETE?
WELL, ANYHOW
I WONDER WHY I FEEL SO INCOMPLETE
SOMETHING'S MISSING, JOE

THE RINK

SOMETHING'S MISSING, PETE
SOMETHING'S MISSING HERE

WHERE ARE MY COLORED LIGHTS?
BEADS AND BLEACHERS AND COLORED LIGHTS?
PASSING SMILES, ROUND AND ROUND
THUMPING OOM PAH PAH ORGAN SOUND
NOISY BOYS, LONG AND LEAN
GIGGLES OF GIRLS IN THE MEZZANINE
FILTERED THROUGH
COLORED LIGHTS
PINK AND YELLOW AND GREEN

AND I TRIED TO FIND THE ANSWER IN THE FRIENDS I MADE, OR BEDS I'D SHARE
(*putting her knapsack on*)
WELL, ANYWHERE
BUT WITH OTHER PEOPLE'S MUSIC RINGING IN MY EAR
I COULDN'T SING
WELL, ANYTHING
(*sitting on the suitcase*)
AND I THOUGHT IF I COULD JUST BE TWELVE AGAIN
OR WAS IT TEN?
WELL, ANYWAY
IT SEEMS TO ME I KNEW THE SECRET THEN
IT'S SO SIMPLE, TWELVE
IT'S SO SIMPLE, TEN
IT'S SO SIMPLE THERE

(*At the same time, we hear the faint, remembered sounds of an amusement park: the merry-go-round and its calliope, the roar of the roller coaster as it thunders by, the happy shouts and laughter of the crowds.*

In the center of the rink, alone in her own special light, is a LITTLE GIRL of 9 or 10. She is wearing roller skates. Very slowly, she will begin to twirl. The movement is graceful, dream-like. Suddenly, she will break out of her twirling pattern and begin to skate around the rink with confident, joyful skating steps.

An electric sign high above the rink has come on: "Everybody Skate." The organ twinkles with its own special lights. It is as if the rink were in full session, even though no one is there but this one LITTLE GIRL who skates and skates and skates.)

PASSING SMILES, ROUND AND ROUND
THUMPING OOM PAH PAH ORGAN SOUND
NOISY BOYS, LONG AND LEAN
GIGGLES OF GIRLS IN THE MEZZANINE
FILTERED THROUGH COLORED LIGHTS
RED AND ORANGE AND GOLD
AND AMBER AND PINK
AND YELLOW AND GREEN

(Suddenly the figure of a YOUNG MAN [GUY/DINO] on skates appears. He is wonderfully handsome and perfect looking. The LITTLE GIRL goes to him. He lifts her high above his head in the most graceful adagio imaginable.

But almost as quickly as he appeared, the YOUNG MAN is gone. The LITTLE GIRL looks after him, then resumes her slow, even spinning movements.)

LEAVING HOME LONG AGO
WHAT WAS I LOOKING FOR?
(*spoken*) I don't know.
   ANNOUNCER. (*offstage*) Last call: Trailways bus, platform three.
   ANGEL. (*singing*)
I CAN'T RECALL
WELL, ANYWAY
SOON I'LL HAVE MY DAYS AND NIGHTS
OF WONDERFUL, GLIMMERING
BEAUTIFUL, SHIMMERING
COLORED LIGHTS!

   [MUSIC CUE 1A: COLORED LIGHTS UNDERSCORE (PLAYOFF)]

(As the song ends, the image of the rink and the LITTLE GIRL will fade. So will the pin spot on ANGEL. For a second the stage is empty and dark.)

THE RINK

[MUSIC CUE 1B: WRECKERS' ENTRANCE]

(*Matter-of-fact worklights have come up in the rink. The illusion, the magic of just a moment ago are gone.*

Instead, we find ourselves in a musty, rundown roller skating establishment that wears its years of neglect none too proudly.

DS.R. *is a curved snack bar, with old fashioned swiveling stools. Just* US. *of the bar is a small exterior access door set into a much larger garage-type door which can be mechanically raised for large deliveries. A staircase* US. *leads up to a balcony, and to a door into the rink owner's apartment. Below, a railing with several gates defines the skating area, which is most of the stage.* DS.L. *is a large dilapidated pipe organ.*

Present are THE WRECKERS, *six men whose job it will be to strip, dismantle and eventually demolish the rink. They are wearing identical overalls with their names stitched over their left breast pockets.* LINO, *who is the crew foreman, is holding the work order on a clipboard. Next to him and looking about the rink with unconcealed admiration is* BEN. LINO *and* BEN *are a good deal older than the other four* WRECKERS.

BUDDY *is a pleasant looking West Indian in his mid-thirties.* LUCKY, *the youngest, will move* DS.L. *to the pipe organ and try to make it sound.* GUY, *the next oldest and clearly the handsomest, is already inspecting the wiring.* TONY, *about the same age as* GUY *and convinced he is God's gift to women, is combing his hair, chewing gum and moving his hips to music that only he can hear.*)

LINO. Hello? (*Music as he crosses in.*) Anybody home? (*BEN moves* US.R., *behind the stairs.* GUY *sits on the trunk stage* R.)
BUDDY. Home? This place? You gotta be kidding. The only thing missing is bats.
GUY. Will you look at the size of this mother? You sure know how to pick 'em, Lino!
LINO. I like a challenge. Anybody can tear a new building down. It's all rinky-tink. These old places put up a fight. (*BEN crosses* DS.L.)

GUY. Yeah, but this one looks like it could win. (*LINO pushes GUY off the trunk and sits on it himself.*)

LINO. That Peanut Farmer in the White House is right: nobody wants to work anymore. (*LINO playfully scatters GUY and BUDDY.*)

LUCKY. (*pulling the plastic drop cloth off the organ*) A real old-fashioned pipe organ! Look at the size of those bass pipes. (*BEN rolls up the plastic and takes it to the trunk. TONY crosses DS.R.*)

TONY. I'll show you a bass pipe!

LUCKY. They're the real thing, Ben.

TONY. (*crossing US.L.*) So's this, sweetheart! (*LUCKY is trying to make the organ sound. GUY is looking around upstairs.*)

BEN. Forget it, Lucky. It's broken. The pipes are all rusted. The stops are all gone.

LUCKY. How much do you think they'd want for something like this? (*GUY comes down the stairs, looking up at the ceiling.*)

BEN. Now what are you gonna do with a broken-down old organ, Lucky?

TONY. The same thing you do with yours, Ben: nothing! I hate organ music. It makes me think I'm dead. Gimme music I can move to.

BEN. People moved to that, Tony.

TONY. What moved? Feet maybe. I'm talking about this. (*He demonstrates with a good thrust of his hips. GUY crosses under the stairs to the wall switches.*)

BEN. Couples skating, a nice waltz, it was lovely.

LINO. You're getting sentimental.

BEN. Someone has to.

LINO. In our line of work that's a—

MEN. (*They've heard it a hundred times.*) Distinct liability.

LINO. All right, ladies! We got a contract to level this place. What we ain't got is—

LUCKY. (*fills in the blank*) All day.

LINO. May we begin? Thank you.

GUY. Heads up! (*He has turned on a sign which reads "GIRLS ONLY" and begun to lower it using the ropes and counterweights.*)

LUCKY. Girls only? What does that mean?

BEN. When that sign came down, the women skated together. No men.

BUDDY. No kidding?

THE RINK

LUCKY. No men?
TONY. No shit? (*GUY turns off the sign.*)
BUDDY. No wonder this place went out of business.
ANNA. (*entering through the apartment door*) You can stop right there. The rink didn't go out of business. I sold it for a lot of money, which is why I'm doing what I'm doing, which is getting the hell out, and you're doing what you're doing, which so far doesn't look like much.
LINO. (*crossing to the bottom of the stairs*) You must be Mrs. Antonelli.
ANNA. Not after today I'm not. (*She holds up the six-pack of beer she has been carrying behind her back.*) I just cleared out my last refrigerator. Now I don't suppose I could interest any of you gentlemen in a beer? (*There is enthusiastic approval from all THE WRECKERS except for LUCKY, who is new at this.*) I didn't think so.
LUCKY. We just got here.
ANNA. What is he? Non-union? (*She comes partway down the stairs and throws a beer to LUCKY. Turning to GUY:*) Here you go, gorgeous.
GUY. No, thanks. I'm on the wagon.
BUDDY. And I'm the one who's gorgeous.
LINO. We're gonna want to start emptying this place out.
ANNA. (*passing out the other beers.*) You can start with that apartment up there. (*BUDDY sits on LUCKY's right on the trunk.*)
BEN. We usually do this after the people are gone.
ANNA. I am gone. Poof! I'm invisible. If I had a stick of dynamite I'd do it myself. (*crossing to* R. *of* C. *stage.*) It may be a little late in my own particular ball game, but I'm giving myself one hell of a ninth inning. (*She opens herself a beer.*) Screw the diet!

[MUSIC CUE 2: CHIEF COOK AND BOTTLE WASHER]

ANNA. (*continued*) To my dear late husband and all his dear late family . . . (*music*) to Antonelli's Roller Rink and Recreation Center . . . I have only one thing to say: (*music*) Va Fangul!
LINO. Let's get moving. (*The men begin to exit through the garage door.*)
GUY. I thought we were on a break.
BEN. Your whole life is a break. (*They are gone.*)

"CHIEF COOK AND BOTTLE WASHER"

Anna.
WHEN I SIT AND REMEMBER THE PAST
THOUGH I'D RATHER NOT SIT AND REMEMBER THE PAST
IF I HAPPEN TO SIT AND REMEMBER THE PAST
I HEAR SO MANY VOICES . . .
Wreckers. (*one by one, from offstage*)
ANNA, ANNA, ANNA, ANNA, ANNA!
Anna.
MASCULINE VOICES
Wrecker 1.
HEY, ANNA, COME UP
Wrecker 2.
HEY, ANNA, COME DOWN
Anna.
HEY, ANNA, DO THIS
HEY, ANNA, DO THAT
Wreckers. (*one by one*)
HEY ANNA, HEY ANNA, HEY ANNA, HEY ANNA, HEY ANNA

Anna. (*spoken*) Stop! I can't be everywhere at once. I'm only one person. Everybody's only one person! (*sung:*)
I WAS RUNNING THE RINK
RUNNING A HOUSEHOLD
AND BEING A WIFE
"WORKING HER ASS OFF"
SHOULD BE THE TITLE OF THE STORY OF MY LIFE

(*VAMP up. The garage door rolls up and the WRECKERS stream through with tools and equipment. Throughout most of the song they are seen crossing back and forth, bringing their things in and removing an odd assortment of objects large and larger.*)

CHIEF COOK AND BOTTLE WASHER
THAT'S WHAT I ALWAYS WAS
DOING WHAT SOME COOK AND BOTTLE WASHER DOES

GO STAND AND TAKE THE TICKETS
GO MAKE THE CORN GO POP

THE RINK

BREAD TO BAKE AND BEDS TO MAKE
AND RUGS TO SHAKE AND FLOORS TO MOP
THEN, WHEN WE BREAK AT SEVEN
UP CLOMPS MY THOUGHTFUL PET
SAYING "HEY, AIN'T MY DINNER READY YET?"
OH, WHAT HEAVEN LIFE CAN BE
WHEN YOU'RE CHIEF COOK AND BOTTLE WASHER
  LIKE ME

CHIEF COOK AND BOTTLE WASHER
THAT'S WHAT I ALWAYS DID
THEN I HAD THE GREAT GOOD LUCK TO HAVE A KID
SO NOW, IT'S WARM THE BOTTLE
SEE WHAT SHE'S CRYING FOR
BATHE AND WIPE AND ROCK AND DIAP
AND BAKE AND TAKE AND MOP AND POP
EXACTLY LIKE I DID BEFORE
THEN, DADDY'S UP AT SEVEN
PEEKS IN THE BASSINET
SAYING, "HEY, AIN'T MY DINNER READY YET?"
OH, WHAT HEAVEN
NOW WE'RE THREE
AND YOU'RE CHIEF COOK AND BOTTLE WASHER
BIG CHIEF COOK AND BOTTLE WASHER
CHIEF COOK, BOTTLE WASHER AND BABY MAKER
  LIKE ME

(*THE WRECKERS have gone for the moment. ANNA pauses to watch the garage door close.*)

BUT NOW, HALLELUJAH, I'M THROUGH
DADDY'S GONE AND THE BABY MAKES TWO
MY TIME?
HELL, IT'S WAY OVERDUE
MY BILLS ARE PAID
MY FUTURE'S MADE

I'M SELLING OFF THIS RATHOLE
I'M GETTING OFF MY KNEES
ON MY WAY AND IN MY PRIME AND AT MY EASE
GO, LET THEM BURN THE BUNTING
LET ALL THE MOPPING STOP

THERE'LL BE NO MORE BREAD TO BAKE
OR BEDS TO MAKE OR FLOORS TO MOP

HEY PORTER, GRAB MY LUGGAGE
I'M GETTIN' ON SOME JET
THEN HEAR *ME* SAY, "HEY, AIN'T MY DINNER READY YET?"
OH, WHAT HEAVEN IT WILL BE
WHEN I GOT COOKS AND BOTTLE WASHERS
A LOAD OF COOKS AND BOTTLE WASHERS
FOR ME!

(*BEN enters from the apartment; LUCKY, TONY, and LINO enter below.*)

BEN. Anything you want in that apartment, you better say so now.
ANNA. It all goes. Except for the suitcases. They come with me.
LINO. Where you going?
ANNA. Rome! Two weeks, first-class!
BEN. That's the way!
TONY. I got an aunt in Naples. (*He heads upstairs with an empty box.*)
ANNA. I'll tell her you said hello.
LINO. You heard the lady! Now move it! Those bulldozers are gonna be here before you know it.

(*BEN and LUCKY follow TONY upstairs and into the apartment. LINO exits via the* US.L. *gate.*)

[MUSIC CUE 2A: ANGEL'S ENTRANCE]

(*The figure of the LITTLE GIRL is seen skating on the rink below. She spins slowly, arching her body gracefully. The YOUNG MAN on skates appears. Again she skates to him. Again he lifts her in a graceful, heart-breaking adagio.*)

ANNA. Angel! Dino!

(*We hear and feel the sounds and vibrations of a roller coaster as it thunders by the rink. It passes directly by. The theatre should shake. Certainly the rink does. As it roars away, the figures of the LITTLE GIRL and YOUNG MAN are gone.*

Suddenly the small outside door US.R. *is opened. We are struck by blinding light, a sense of blue sky, a feeling of the ocean and boardwalk that are right outside. It is the first time that we have been made aware of them.*

The audience, like ANNA, will need a moment to see who has come in through the blinding light.

It is ANGEL. She is dressed as before. She carries two suitcases and wears a knapsack.)

ANNA. (*turning, squinting into the light*) I'm closed. (*ANGEL takes a step forward.*) I said we're closed!

(*ANGEL closes the door. The closed-off, claustrophobic atmosphere of the rink is quickly re-established.*)

ANGEL. (*leaning on the* US. *door frame*) It's me, Ma.
ANNA. Jesus.

(*The roller coaster thunders by again. It is impossible to speak over its noise. ANNA and ANGEL just look at one another.*)

ANGEL. (*nervously laughing; half-trying to make herself heard over the coaster; half-knowing it's hopeless*) Home sweet home! The Red Devil! (*The roller coaster fades away.*) Well some things never change. (*crossing to* L. *of* C.) Hi, Ma. (*pause*) Hello to you, too.
ANNA. What are you doing here?
ANGEL. Nothing. (*at a loss*) I was in the neighborhood.
ANNA. (*acknowledging the bags*) With all that?
ANGEL. I've been traveling. I thought I'd see how you were.
ANNA. I'm fine.
ANGEL. So am I. I thought you'd never ask.
ANNA. What were you expecting? A welcome sign?
ANGEL. Don't worry, I wasn't expecting anything. (*She puts her bags down.*) Two seconds in the door and it starts.
ANNA. (*crossing to* C. *stage.*) You know certain outfits trigger

me. Did you have to come home wearing all ten of 'em?

ANGEL. I've been on a bus for three days. The last two the toilet was out. Gimme a break.

ANNA. (*crossing below ANGEL to* R. *of center*) She comes all the way from California to use the john.

ANGEL. I came home to see if there was any hope for us.

ANNA. Us? You and me us? Don't worry about me. I work solo. I have for a long time.

ANGEL. (*taking off her knapsack*) So have I. I thought maybe it was about time we tried to change that. I got a lot of things to tell you, Ma.

ANNA. You can start by telling me the story behind the hair.

ANGEL. What story?

ANNA. The color, for openers.

ANGEL. This is my color.

ANNA. This is your mother.

ANGEL. Look who's talking!

ANNA. A little rinse. I never denied it.

ANGEL. Hah!

ANNA. May God strike you dead if I ever once denied subtly coloring my hair.

ANGEL. May God strike *me* dead?

ANNA. You know what I mean! Can we change the subject? (*ANNA crosses* DS.R.)

ANGEL. Gladly. (*She will sit on her suitcase and start looking for something in her knapsack.*)

ANNA. (*turning back to ANGEL*) If you got something for me in there, forget it. Don't think you can soften me up with a little gift. You got that from your father.

ANNA. This isn't for you. (*She is unwrapping a candy bar.*)

ANNA. All I ever got from you is postcards. "Dear Ma, California is great. I'm living in a community."

ANGEL. That's commune.

ANNA. Sounded like musical beds to me.

ANGEL. They were. Why do you think they were so popular? (*She crosses* DS.L.)

ANNA. (*crossing above ANGEL to stage* L.) "Dear Ma, greetings from Seattle! I got arrested in a protest march."

ANGEL. (*moving* C. *stage*) Along with six hundred other people. It wasn't anything personal.

ANNA. (*coming* DS.R.) "Dear Ma, greetings from Colorado." This one's my favorite. "I'm working with the Indians. They're people, too." I could have told you that one, Pocohantas.

ANGEL. (*sitting on her suitcase*) I'm not going to let you get me mad this time. (*She takes a bite of her candy bar.*)

ANNA. She still stuffs.

ANGEL. She's a grown woman, Ma.

ANNA. (*crossing around ANGEL to stage* L.) I can see where she's grown.

ANGEL. I only eat when I'm nervous.

ANNA. Then you've been nervous for 29 years.

ANGEL. Try 30.

ANNA. You're not 30.

ANGEL. Of course I'm 30.

ANGEL. You're 29.

ANGEL. Ma, I oughta know.

ANNA. I'm your mother. There is no way I have a 30 year old child. (*ANNA has taken one of ANGEL's munchies.*)

ANGEL. You're not making this any easier for me, Ma.

ANNA. Easy?

[MUSIC CUE 3: DON'T AH MA ME]

I'll tell you what's easy. Vanishing off the face of the earth. (*music*) That's easy. Staying here is what was hard. (*music up*)

ANGEL. I'm here now, aren't I? (*She gets up and crosses* DS.R. *to ANNA's left.*)

ANNA. You're too late.

ANGEL. Ah, Ma.

ANNA. How long was it this time? Seven years!

ANGEL. Ah, Ma.

ANNA. Basta. Finito. That's it. We're closed. (*She sees one of ANGEL's munchies in her hand.*) Now look what you've made me do.

ANGEL. Ah, Ma. (*ANNA and ANGEL sing:*)

"DON'T AH MA ME"

ANNA.
IF THE EARTH HAD OPENED UP
IF IT SWALLOWED ME INSIDE
WOULD MY DARLING BABY GIRL
EVEN REALIZE I'D DIED?
YOU WERE SITTING ON A HILL

WITH SOME YIPPIE ON YOUR LAP
TALKING LOVE AND LIFE AND ART
AND THAT TRANSCENDENTAL CRAP
WITH THE DOPE I'M SURE YOU SMOKE
AND A HEALTHY DOSE OF COKE
UP YOUR NOSE
    Angel.
AH MA
    Anna.
UP YOUR NOSE
    Angel.
(*crossing* c., *away from ANNA*)
AH MA
    Anna.
(*following ANGEL to* L. *stage*)
AND FOR ALL YOU EVER KNEW
I WAS HUSTLING FOR THE RENT
'CAUSE YOU ONLY CALLED COLLECT
MAYBE EVERY OTHER LENT
(*crossing back to* c.)
WHILE I'M BLEEDING ON THE STREET
FROM SOME MANIAC'S ATTACK
YOU'RE IN SOME RAMADA INN
SEEKING WISDOM ON YOUR BACK
MAKING KIBBLE OF YOUR BRAIN
AN EMANCIPATED PAIN
IN THE ASS
    Angel.
AH MA.
    Anna.
(*crossing* L., *around ANGEL*)
IN THE ASS
    Angel.
(*following ANNA* L.)
AH MA
    Anna.
(*backing ANGEL to* c.)
AND DON'T AH MA ME
YOU SAID YOU HAD TO FIND YOURSELF
SO FIND YOURSELF SOME OTHER PLACE
AND DON'T AH MA ME
I DON'T NEED YOU AROUND
TO HELP ME COMPLICATE MY LIFE

AND IF YOU REALLY GAVE A DAMN
YOU'D HAVE NEVER STAYED AWAY
WHEN YOU BREAK A MOTHER'S HEART
DOES IT MAKE A GURU'S DAY?
BUT YOU'RE NEARLY THIRTY NOW
AND YOU'RE PANICKED AND UPSET
SO YOU WALK BACK IN THE DOOR
AND EXPECT ME TO FORGET
WELCOME HOME, MY LITTLE PIG
BOY, YOU REALLY GOT A BIG
SET OF BALLS

   ANGEL.
AH MA
   ANNA.
(*crossing* L.)
SOME BALLS
   ANGEL.
(*following*)
AH MA
   ANNA.
(*backing ANGEL to* C.)
AND DON'T AH MA ME
YOU SAID YOU HAD TO FIND YOURSELF
SO FIND YOURSELF SOME OTHER PLACE
AND DON'T AH MA ME
I DON'T NEED YOU AROUND
(*looking at the candy bar*)
TO HELP ME COMPLICATE MY LIFE
CAPISCE?

DON'T AH MA ME
THE SIGN ON THE APARTMENT
DOESN'T SAY "SALVATION ARMY" DOES IT?
DON'T AH MA ME
I'VE HEARD IT ALL YOUR LIFE
AND I DON'T NEED TO HEAR IT NOW
(*crossing down* R.)

   ANGEL.
AH MA
   ANNA. (*spoken*) Jesus!
   ANGEL. (*crossing* L.)
IT'S LIKE IT WAS BEFORE

I JUST WALK THROUGH THE DOOR
AND RIGHT AWAY YOU START TO FIGHT AND CURSE
    Anna.
THAT'S BULLSHIT!
    Angel. (*moving* c. *and sitting on the suitcase*)
MA, I HOPED THERE'D BE SOME TEARS
AND AFTER ALL THESE YEARS
YOU MIGHT HAVE MELLOWED SOME
BUT JESUS, WAS I DUMB
    Anna. (*crossing to ANGEL*)
SO YOU THOUGHT I MIGHT BE CALM
MAYBE JOLLY YOU ALONG
BUT BELIEVE ME I'M NOT CALM
AND BELIEVE ME YOU WERE WRONG
SHOULD THE SOUND OF YOUR HELLO
BE LIKE MUSIC TO MY EARS
(*crossing behind ANGEL to* L.)
WHEN I HAVEN'T SEEN YOUR FACE
IN, WHAT IS IT, SEVEN YEARS?
NOW YOU WALK BACK IN MY LIFE
SHOULD I REALLY BLESS MY LUCK?
THAT'S AN OUTFIT YOU COULD WEAR
ON A SANITATION TRUCK
HAVE A DAUGHTER, I WAS TOLD
THEY'RE A BLESSING WHEN YOU'RE OLD
AH, STROONGATZ
    Angel.
(*She stands and crosses down* L.)
AH MA
    Anna.
STROONGATZ
    Angel.
AH MA
    Anna.
ENOUGH
    Angel.
AH MA
    Anna.
THAT'S IT
    Angel.
AH MA

Anna.
SHUT UP
 Angel.
AH MA
 Anna.
I QUIT
 Angel.
AH MA—
 Anna.
NOW I GOT A GOOD THING GOING
AND I DON'T NEED YOU TO HEX IT
DID YOU NOTICE WHERE YOU ENTER
YOU CAN ALSO MAKE AN EXIT?

SO GO OUT AND FIND A HUSBAND
JOIN A CONVENT
BE A WHORE
BUT I AM SICK AND TIRED OF YOUR
AH MA
 Angel.
AH MA
 Anna.
Ssshh!

Angel. Ssshh? That's it? Just ssshh? We're having a breakthrough in our relationship. The last time I was home you told me to drop dead.

Anna. (*crossing* DS.R.) I did not.

Angel. (*crossing to ANNA*) "Drop dead" you told me.

Anna. I would never tell my only child to "Drop dead." "Go to hell" maybe but not "Drop dead."

Angel. I give up! (*She goes to her suitcase.*)

Anna. That's right: have another brownie.

Angel. It's not a brownie. It's a Cranberry Granola Bran Date Bar. I'm into health food. (*She bends over the suitcase.*)

Anna. You're barely into those pants. Look at you.

Angel. (*crossing* US.L. *of the suitcase*) I'm going on a diet tomorrow.

Anna. How *this* produced *that* . . . !

Angel. Don't take *all* the credit. I must have gotten something from him.

Anna. All you ever got from your father was sand in your shoes.

[MUSIC CUE 4: BLUE CRYSTAL]

(*more quietly, to herself*) All *I* ever got from him was sand in my face.

(*A special light has come up on DINO ANTONELLI [GUY]. It is 1950 and DINO is the kind of young man a young woman could die from. He is behind the bar and is hiding something behind his back.*)

ANGEL. (*still in "the present"*) That and me.
DINO. (*to ANNA*) Close your eyes!
ANNA. No games, Dino, I'm mad at you.
DINO. Are they closed?
ANGEL. What I really got from him was my incredible charm.
DINO. I said, close your eyes.
ANNA. (*after a beat, she closes them.*) I mean it. You were gone three days this time. (*DINO sings:*)

"BLUE CRYSTAL"

DINO.
WAS IT THREE DAYS? ONLY THREE DAYS? THAT'S AMAZING!
ANGEL. He could talk you into anything.
ANNA. What the hell are you talking about?
DINO.
ALL THAT WAY IN THREE DAYS? THAT'S AMAZING!

(*Still holding his hands behind his back, he crosses* DS.R. *to ANNA.*)

ANNA. Stop turning things around, will ya?
DINO.
I ONLY WENT BECAUSE OF YOU
I WENT TO BUY YOU SOMETHING BEAUTIFUL
IT WAS A LONG, EXHAUSTING TRIP
BUT I FIGURED YOU WERE WORTH IT
STILL . . . ONLY THREE DAYS! THAT'S PERFECTLY AMAZING!
ANNA. All right, I'll bite. Where've you been? (*ANNA chases DINO* L. *past ANGEL, who is in ANNA's way.*)

Dino.
I'VE BEEN TO THE MOON AND BACK
AND YOU KNOW WHAT THEY'VE GOT UP THERE?
BLUE CRYSTAL
(*DINO runs back to the bar, jumps up and sits on top with his feet on the* DS. *stool.* ANNA *follows him. He reveals the goblets in his hands.*)

ANNA. That's very poetic, Dino. And they're beautiful. But where did you buy them? What store? Come on.

DINO. You can't just walk in a store and buy something like this. You got to know somebody. (*ANGEL sits on the suitcase.*)

ANNA. (*sitting on the bar next to* DINO) I know who you know. So, who do you know?

DINO.
I MET A MAN ON THE MOON WHO SITS AROUND ALL DAY
AND HE SHAPES BLUE CRYSTAL

HE'S GOT A FURNACE AND A BLOWER AND A MALLET AND A CHISEL
AND HE SHAPES BLUE CRYSTAL

SO I SAID, I WANT A PRESENT FOR A VERY SPECIAL LADY
THAT YOU CAN'T BUY IN A STORE
SO HE SOLD ME EIGHT GOBLETS AND THERE AREN'T ANY MORE
IN THE WHOLE WIDE WORLD

YES, I'VE BEEN TO THE MOON
(*He pours liquid from one goblet to another.*)
AND I BROUGHT YOU BACK
BLUE CRYSTAL
(*He turns the full goblet upside-down; magically glitter falls.*)

ANNA. (*leaving the bar and crossing* R. *of* C.) I'm pregnant, Dino.

DINO. (*after a beat*) Why do you think I went all the way to the moon and back to get you those?

(*As the music ends, the light fades on* DINO, *who exits below the snack bar. We are back in "the present."* LINO,

> LUCKY, TONY, and BUDDY have appeared. LINO emerges from behind the bar with the box of blue crystal goblets. He sets the box on the US. end of the bar and takes one glass out.)

ANGEL. Him and his magic.
LINO. Say, Mrs. Antonelli, what about these?
ANGEL. Somebody's talking to you, Ma.
ANNA. (*quickly recovering*) What is it?
LINO. I'll give you ten bucks a glass for 'em.
ANGEL. What are you doing?
ANNA. What does it look like?
ANGEL. You just told me they were from him.
ANNA. I'm allergic to blue. (*ANGEL takes the glass from LINO.*)
ANGEL. No, I'm taking these.
LINO. Who are you?
ANGEL. Her daughter. Who are you?
LINO. Her hairdresser. What does it look like?

(*During the above exchange, BUDDY has come on* DS.L. *with 4 coke cases, which he places below the stairs, and then exits* R. *LUCKY has come down the stairs with 2 lamps, which he carries out the right door. LINO, having emerged from the* US. *side of the bar, follows the others out.*)

ANGEL. (*putting the glass back in the box*) Who was that? (*She crosses* US. *with the box to below the stairs and places it on top of the crates.*)
ANNA. You mean his name? I don't know. They're usually Tony or something.
ANGEL. (*coming* DS.) What are they doing here?
ANNA. (*at* L. *of* C.) I'm getting rid of a few things. Junk.
ANGEL. (*going back to the crates and holding up a glass*) You call this junk?

[MUSIC CUE 4A: BLUE CRYSTAL/KOREA]

You don't just walk into a store and buy a glass like this. You gotta know somebody. You really are crazy.

(*The lighting changes abruptly, plunging us into 1952. DINO bursts through the apartment door and comes down the stairs.*)

DINO. What are you? Crazy?
ANNA. Crazy! (*She turns* US. *to look at DINO.*) I'll show you crazy.
ANGEL. (*still in "the present," with a glass in her hand*) There used to be eight of these.
ANNA. Who is she? (*DINO also has one of the goblets. He crosses with it to the snackbar.*)
DINO. Every time you ask me, Anna, I'm gonna break one.
ANNA. I'll kill her. I'll find you both and tear her heart out.
DINO. There is no one else.
ANNA. Liar!
DINO. (*crossing behind the bar*) I swear it.
ANNA. (*crossing right to the bar*) Liar! Who is she? (*DINO raises the goblet to smash it. ANGEL, crossing DS.L., is both observer and participant.*)
ANGEL. I don't want to hear this.
DINO. How long has she been standing there?
ANNA. Go to your room.
DINO. It's okay, Angel.
ANNA. It's not okay. I said go to your room.
DINO. Don't yell at her.
ANNA. I'm not yelling!
ANGEL. (*at* DS.L.) I got scared up there. . . .
DINO. You see, Anna, you see?
ANNA. No, *you* see! (*She crosses* US.R. *and gets the box of blue crystal glasses.*)

(*DINO's FATHER [BEN] appears.*)

DINO'S FATHER. (*annoyed by the sounds of their argument*) What's wrong with you? The two of you! (*He sees ANGEL.*) In front of the . . . ! (*He turns away, disgusted.*)
DINO. I can't take this. I'm gonna enlist. It'll do us both good.

(*ANGEL crosses* US.C., *following the curve of the set, and continues* US.R. *of the snackbar. She is looking at the glass in her hand as if watching the past.*)

ANNA. (*putting the box of glasses on the bar*) He wants to go to Korea now and get himself killed your wonderful only son! (*She takes out a glass and wraps it in newspaper.*)

DINO'S FATHER. (*crossing to the* US.C. *gate*) It's time to open up, Dino.

(*DINO's FRIENDS are heard calling him off.*)

DINO'S FRIENDS. (*offstage*) Dino! Hey, Dino!
DINO. (*crossing below the bar to* R. *of* C.) I gotta go. America's calling me.
DINO'S FATHER. It'll do him good.
ANNA. Dino!
DINO. (*at the stage* R. *door*) I'll be back. It's only a war. (*He goes.*)
DINO'S FATHER. (*at the* US.C. *gate*) Anna, open the snack bar.

(*He goes. Light change. It is 1978. The music has stopped. ANGEL is at the bar, still holding the glass.*)

ANNA. You don't want those.
ANGEL. (*unwrapping another glass*) Speak for yourself.
ANNA. You can't put 'em in your dishwasher.
ANGEL. Ma, does this look like a woman with a dishwasher? (*She crosses* C. *to her bags, and starts with them towards the stairs.*)
ANNA. (*re-wrapping a glass*) What are you going to do with 'em? Carry 'em around in that knapsack? Now where are you going?
ANGEL. To my room. I'm thinking of staying this time.
ANNA. How long? (*ANGEL stops at the bottom of the stairs and puts her bags down.*)
ANGEL. I don't know. Just maybe the rest of my life.
ANNA. What brought this on? Or shouldn't I ask?

[MUSIC CUE 5: FAMILIAR THINGS]

ANGEL. (*taking her coat off and crossing* L. *of* C.) I *know:* this place used to be everything I wanted to run away from.
ANNA. (*wrapping another glass*) Don't worry. You did.
ANGEL. What did you expect from me? It was the sixties.

Everybody with a mother ran away. Besides, I didn't know what we had here. (*Now she wraps a glass.*) I took all this for granted. I mean, who *didn't* live in an amusement park? (*She puts the glass in the box.*)

Angel.
UNDER THE ROLLER COASTER
NEXT TO THE JUNGLE RIDE
RIGHT OF THE CATERPILLAR
LEFT OF THE WATER SLIDE
BACK OF THE SILVER STREAK
IN FRONT OF THE WHIP
TWO BLOCKS FROM CASEY'S INTERPLANETARY TRIP

Anna. (*leaning on the bar*) Angel, listen. (*ANGEL moves to the bar and sits on a stool.*)

Angel.
FAMILIAR THINGS
THE THINGS ABOUT FAMILIAR THINGS
IS HOW YOU KEEP IMAGINING
THEY'LL NEVER GO AWAY
THEY'RE NOTHING SPECIAL
(*rising and crossing c.*)
THEY'VE ALWAYS BEEN THERE
AND SO YOU REALLY DON'T APPRECIATE FAMILIAR THINGS

Anna. (*crossing around the DS. end of the bar*) Angel, I gotta tell you something.

Angel. I don't have any other place to go, Ma. This is the only thing I've got right now. This is it. The end of the line. I can't run anymore and I'm tired, real tired. I need a place to be, Mama. (*ANNA crosses US. and sits on the crates. ANGEL sits at the DS. end of the bar.*)

Angel.
FAMILIAR THINGS
THE THING ABOUT FAMILIAR THINGS
IS HOW YOU KEEP IMAGINING
THEY'LL NEVER GO AWAY
YOU TAKE FOR GRANTED
THE WARMTH THEY BRING YOU
AND SO YOU REALLY DON'T APPRECIATE FAMILIAR THINGS
(*She rises and crosses DS.L.*)

BUT HERE I AM
AGAIN AMONG FAMILIAR THINGS
AND FINDING WHAT THEY MEAN TO ME
THE EVIDENCE IS CLEAR
YOUR LIFE IS FILLED WITH STRINGS
CONNECTED TO FAMILIAR THINGS
AND ALL OF MINE ARE HERE
(*sitting on the organ bench*)
UNDER THE ROLLER COASTER
NEXT TO THE JUNGLE RIDE
RIGHT OF THE CATERPILLAR
LEFT OF THE WATER SLIDE
(*ANGEL is trying to make the organ sound. Spoken:*) What happened to the organ?

Anna. It died two years before I closed the snack bar. (*crossing* C.) I'm trying to tell you, Angel. It's all shot. The light board, the sound system, the plumbing. You think your bus was bad? Try our ladies' room.

Angel. (*jumping up*) We'll fix it. (*coming* C.) That's what I'm talking about!

Anna. Go back where you came from, Angel. (*crossing* R.) There's nothing here for you.

Angel. (*crossing to the stairs*) I don't see the glitter ball. Where's the glitter ball—? (*She crosses half-way upstairs, trying to see the glitter ball.*)

Anna. It's broken, too. (*She crosses behind the bar, and puts away the box of glasses.*)

Angel. I see cobwebs, crud. What have you done to this place?

Anna. Something I should have done twenty-five years ago.

Angel. Answer me!

Anna. Ssshh! You want them to hear? (*She jabs her finger in the direction of THE WRECKERS.*)

Angel. The glitter ball was mine. He gave it to me.

Anna. You're not a child any more, Angel.

[MUSIC CUE 5A: BLUE CRYSTAL UNDERSCORE]

(*Light change. DINO appears at the small right door. He is dressed in his Army uniform. He is drunk and in boisterous high spirits. It is late at night. It is 1953.*)

Dino. Angel! (*He runs half-way upstairs, past ANGEL, who*

now observes the scene without being a part of it.)
 ANNA. (*crossing around the* DS. *edge of the bar*) I mean it.
 DINO. Angel!
 ANNA. You'll wake her. The party was this afternoon.
 DINO. I know. Where the hell were you?

(*He laughs uproariously. LENNY [LINO], HIRAM [BUDDY], an army buddy, TOM [TONY], another army buddy, and SUGAR [LUCKY], Tom's date, enter from the stage* R. *door. They have all clearly been partying with DINO.*)

 LENNY. (*crossing to the bar with a yellow shopping bag*) Hi, Anna, we're sorry.
 DINO. (*moving to the left of Lenny;* ANNA *is at the* DS.R. *stool*) This is Lenny, Anna. That's right. He wanted to marry you.
 LENNY. (*crossing* DS.R.) Come on, Dino, don't.
 DINO. (*to the others*) Lenny here didn't go to Korea. He stayed behind to take care of his mommy and make goo goo eyes at my wife while I was over there defending the I-don't-know-what-the-hell-I-was-defending but I sure (*crossing* L.) defended the hell out of it?
 ANNA. I'll get some coffee. (*She moves* R. *to exit—DINO grabs her by the right hand and pulls her back.*)
 DINO. Say hello to my friends. (*crossing* C. *with ANNA*) This is Hiram. Hiram and me were like this.
 HIRAM. You better believe it.
 DINO. And this is Tom Bellaggio. Another great guy.
 TOM. Battaglia. (*He shakes hands with ANNA.*) Tom Battaglia.
 DINO. You're still a great guy. And this is Tom's lovely lady of the evening . . . I mean lady for the evening . . . what's your name, honey?
 SUGAR. Sugar. Just Sugar. Hi, Mrs. Antonelli, it's a pleasure.
 DINO. Doesn't Sugar have great teeth?
 SUGAR. You should have seen him! The life of the party!
 ANNA. (*crossing* R. *to the* DS. *end of the bar*) What party?
 SUGAR. (*crosses* R. *to the* US. *end of the bar. TOM joins her.*) I mean—I'm sorry.

(*DINO's FATHER has entered from the apartment and has come down the stairs.*)

DINO'S FATHER. Dino!

DINO. And this is—oh, Christ—my father.

DINO'S FATHER. (*crossing* C. *to DINO*) Dino, this is our home!

DINO. What home? It's a goddamn roller rink. (*crossing to the stairs*) Angel! Where's my little girl?

ANNA. Let her sleep.

DINO. It's her goddamn birthday. I got a goddamn present for her. (*ANGEL steps into the scene, moving partway down the stairs.*)

ANGEL. Daddy?

DINO. There she is. What did I tell you? (*He brings ANGEL down the stairs.*) Is that an angel? Say hello to my friends, honey. Show 'em how nice and polite you are.

ANGEL. Hello.

SUGAR. She's beautiful, Dino.

DINO. What did you expect?

LENNY. (*rescuing ANGEL*) Happy birthday, Angel.

ANGEL. Uncle Lenny. You brought Uncle Lenny! (*She comes* DS.R. *to LENNY and hugs him.*)

DINO. (*laughing for the others*) Uncle!

LENNY. How old are you?

ANGEL. Five.

DINO. (*Jealous of LENNY, he takes ANGEL's hand and brings her* C. *stage.*) What did you tell me you wanted for your birthday?

ANGEL. (*shyly*) You know.

DINO. Tell me again.

ANGEL. They'll hear.

DINO. So?

DINO'S FATHER. You're scaring her, Dino.

DINO. Scare my own little girl! Are you scared of me, honey?

[MUSIC CUE 6: NOT ENOUGH MAGIC]

ANGEL. (*uncertainly*) No.

DINO. (*kneeling next to ANGEL*) Tell me again. Tell Daddy what you want.

ANGEL. (*pushing ANNA away and kneeling on the floor with DINO*) But just you. (*She whispers in his ear. DINO's eyes widen in amazement. He is quite irresistible when he plays with her like this. LENNY takes ANNA's hand.*)

DINO. Is that what you want? (*ANGEL nods. To the others:*)

She wants magic. (*getting up*) My kid wants magic. (*He crosses* L. *ANGEL follows.*)
 ANGEL. You told them! (*DINO's FATHER takes her hand.*)
 DINO. You know something? She's absolutely right. (*LENNY sits at the bar. DINO sings:*)

"NOT ENOUGH MAGIC"

DINO.
THERE'S NOT ENOUGH MAGIC
NOT ENOUGH SPARKLE
NOT ENOUGH WONDER
NOT ENOUGH GLITTER
NOT ENOUGH HOCUS POCUS ANYMORE

(*He crosses* L. *to ANNA.*)
THERE'S NOT ENOUGH ROMANCE
NOT ENOUGH TOUCHING
NOT ENOUGH HOLDING
NOT ENOUGH MUSIC
NOT ENOUGH COUPLES WALTZING 'ROUND THE FLOOR

(*DINO's FATHER will cross to the organ. DINO runs around ANGEL* DS.C. *and kneels on her* R.)

DINO. (*continued*)
THERE'S NOT ENOUGH BIRTHDAYS
NOT ENOUGH EASTER
NOT ENOUGH LAUGHTER
NOT ENOUGH TICKLING
NOT ENOUGH CANDY IN THE CANDY STORE

NOW, SOME PEOPLE SAY THAT'S FOOLISH
THEY TELL ME IT DOESN'T MATTER
BUT I SAY, "THERE'S NOT ENOUGH MAGIC"
(*He ends* US.R. *of* C., *near HIRAM.*)
 ANGEL. I don't see any magic, Papa.
 DINO. You don't? Well, let's see if we can make some. Close your eyes, sugar . . . Are they closed?
 ANGEL. Yes. (*He pushes a large box* C. *stage. LENNY crosses*

to the US. *end of the bar and passes out flashlights from the yellow bag.*)

DINO. Papa. (*DINO's FATHER plays a fanfare on the organ.*) Anna, turn out the lights. (*ANNA crosses to the bar and reaches behind to turn off the rink lights.*) Hiram. (*HIRAM turns on a flashlight and shines it on the box. One by one, the others follow suit.*) Lenny! Tony!
TOM. It's Tom.
DINO. (*good natured*) Shut up! What's-your-name! Teeth! (*turning his own flashlight on*) And now me!

(*He crosses* DS. *to ANGEL and brings her* US.C., *positioning her to the left of the box.*

At DINO's signal, the box flies open—possibly with an explosion and puff of smoke—revealing a brand new, wonderfully large glitter ball.

A cable descends and they hook it up to the magic ball.

DINO turns on the big spotlights. The glitter ball begins to spin, and then rise. A magical moment.)

ANNA. (*looking up at the glitter ball*) It's beautiful. (*crossing* C. *to DINO*) I'm sorry I was cross. I guess I'm not used to having you back yet.
DINO. We'll talk later on. This is for Angel.

(*HIRAM pulls the empty box* US., *then moves to the stairs. SUGAR crosses* R. *of* C. *DINO's FATHER leaves the organ. DINO sings:*)

(*crossing* R., US. *of the ball*)
'ROUND IT GOES, ROUND IT GOES
JUST LIKE THE EARTH
 ANGEL.
ONLY MUCH MORE BEAUTIFUL
 DINO.
'ROUND IT GOES, 'ROUND IT GOES
JUST LIKE THE WORLD
 ANGEL. (*crossing left of the ball*)
ONLY MUCH MORE BEAUTIFUL

DINO.
TURN, TURN, GLITTER AND TWIRL
LIGHT UP THE EYES OF MY LITTLE GIRL
SHINE LIKE STARS IN THE SNOW
   ANGEL & DINO.
ONLY MUCH MORE BEAUTIFUL
   DINO. May I have this waltz, young lady?

(*The others sing as they dance.*)

   HIRAM.
ONLY MUCH MORE BEAUTIFUL
   HIRAM, SUGAR, DINO'S FATHER, LENNY.
'ROUND IT GOES, 'ROUND IT GOES
JUST LIKE THE WORLD
ONLY MUCH MORE BEAUTIFUL
TURN, TURN, GLITTER AND TWIRL
LIGHT UP THE EYES OF SOME LITTLE GIRL
SHINE LIKE STARS IN THE SNOW
   HIRAM.
ONLY MUCH MORE BEAUTIFUL

(*After dancing with ANGEL, DINO moves from R. to C. stage. ANNA comes to him.*)

   ANNA. (*ready to dance with DINO*) You know how long it's been since you asked me to dance?
   DINO. Dance with Tom. He's terrific.
   ANNA. I want to dance with you, Dino.
   DINO. I'm too bombed.
   ANNA. We'll fake it!

(*She takes him into her arms and dances with him. HIRAM and SUGAR begin a Lindy. LENNY, TOM, and even ANGEL join in.*

DINO's FATHER, having exited with the glitter ball box US.C., returns during the dance with a tray of 8 blue crystal glasses and crosses to the bar, where he will open and pour champagne.

DINO soon pulls away from ANNA, having had enough, and

insists that TOM take over. While DINO sits brooding at the bar, ANNA and TOM dance a smouldering pas de deux to the cool jazz. He is terrific and so is ANNA. Suddenly the music turns hot and SUGAR, HIRAM, and LENNY break into a wild jazz improvisation with ANNA and TOM at the center.

The dance ends with cheers and hugs exchanged by everyone except DINO. DINO's FATHER passes out champagne in the blue Venetian glass goblets.)

ANNA. Make a wish, honey.
ANGEL. I wish . . .
ANNA. It's got to be a secret.
OTHERS. Speech! Speech!
ANGEL. I have the best daddy in the whole world and this is the most beautiful rink in the whole, whole world and we're all gonna be here like this forever and ever.
SUGAR. I'll drink to that, kid.
DINO. Nothing's forever, Angel.
SUGAR. There's always a wet blanket. (*DINO will rise and cross behind the bar.*)
ANNA. Your papa is wrong. Some things are forever. Your papa's forever, I'm forever, we're forever, the rink's forever.
DINO'S FATHER.
HERE'S TO THE RINK
AND ALL OF US TOGETHER
AND ALL OF US TOGETHER
LET'S DRINK TO THAT
ANNA.
I'LL DRINK TO THAT
ANGEL.
I'LL DRINK TO THAT
HIRAM.
I'LL DRINK TO THAT
TOM & SUGAR.
I'LL DRINK TO THAT
ALL.
I'LL DRINK TO THAT
ALL.
I'LL DRINK TO THAT
I'LL DRINK TO THAT

ANNA. Dino?
DINO. I'll drink to that.

(*Suddenly DINO explodes in frustration and anger and smashes one of the blue crystal glasses. NOTE: a "crash box" should be mounted behind the bar to catch the glass.*)

ANNA. (*running to the bar*) Dino!
DINO'S FATHER. (*crossing to the US. end of the bar*) What's the matter with you?
DINO. Leave me alone!

(*He swings around and accidently slaps her.*)

[MUSIC CUE 7: WE CAN MAKE IT]

(*It is a moment of pain, confusion and drunken shame. LENNY starts towards ANNA, but stops as he sees ANGEL. ANNA leans over the bar to hug DINO. The "party" starts to break up, everyone leaving their glasses on the tray on the bar.*)

TOM. Come on, we'll drive back into the city. Dominic's'll still be open.
SUGAR. (*getting her stole from the bar*) What got into him? (*TOM, SUGAR, and HIRAM go out the right door.*)
LENNY. Happy birthday, Angel. (*He gives her a teddy bear from the shopping bag and follows the others out.*)
DINO'S FATHER. It's that war over there. It changed him. Come with your grandpops, Angel.

(*He takes the teddy bear and glass from ANGEL and leads her as far as the top of the stairs. He exits into the apartment. ANGEL watches her mother and father, who are DS. of the bar.*)

DINO. I don't know what's wrong, Anna. It all used to be so . . . Everything fit. (*He drops to the floor between two stools.*)
ANNA. It's not easy, coming back.
DINO. All of a sudden nothing's the same. I'm scared.
ANNA. (*sitting on the floor DS.R. of DINO*) It's okay. I'm right here for you. (*ANNA sings:*)

"WE CAN MAKE IT"

ANNA.
PEOPLE MAY HURT US
WE CAN TAKE IT
HERE COMES A BAD DAY
WE CAN SHAKE IT
I'M WITH YOU, YOU'RE WITH ME
WE CAN MAKE IT

(*DINO has crawled to ANNA. He puts his head in her lap.*)

SOME LITTLE QUARREL
WE'LL GET THROUGH IT
LOVE ISN'T EASY
WE CAN DO IT
YOU AND ME
WAIT AND SEE
WE CAN MAKE IT

(*She strokes DINO's head.*)

LONG AS I KNOW YOU'RE TRYING
LONG AS I KNOW YOU CARE
LONG AS WE STICK TOGETHER
WE'LL TAKE ON ANYONE,
ANYTIME, ANYWHERE

(*They kiss. DINO sits up, and ANNA holds his face in her hands.*)

I HAVE YOU
YOU HAVE ME
WE CAN MAKE IT
RIGHT TO THE END OF ALWAYS
DOWN TO THE FINISH LINE
WE CAN MAKE IT
FINE!

ANGEL. Ma!
DINO. (*rising and crossing* C.) She's calling you.
ANNA. (*rising*) Not now, Angel. (*ANNA and DINO start dancing again.*)
ANGEL. Ma!

Anna. I said not now. (*sings:*)
THEY NEVER MADE A TOWER
WE WERE TOO WEAK TO CLIMB
LONG AS WE PULL TOGETHER
WE'LL TAKE ON ANYTHING
ANYWHERE, ANYTIME
(*embracing him*)

I HAVE YOU
YOU HAVE ME
WE CAN MAKE IT
RIGHT TO THE END OF ALWAYS
DOWN TO THE FINISH LINE
WE CAN MAKE IT
FINE!

(*DINO vanishes from her embrace, exiting behind the bar.*

Suddenly the glitter ball comes crashing down. It will stop on its cable only a few inches from shattering on the rink floor. It has almost hit ANNA, but ANGEL has run down the stairs and pushed her out of the way. At the same time, the work lights have come on. The rink quickly returns to its drab, run-down look.

BUDDY is on the platform above, holding the mirror-ball ropes. BEN, LUCKY, TONY, and LINO have entered variously below.)

Lino. Easy with that!
Angel. Look out, Ma!
Lino. I said easy! What's the matter with you?
Anna. All you had to do was ask me to move. I would've moved.
Angel. Are you okay?
Anna. Fine.
Buddy. I'm sorry.
Angel. Drop a three hundred pound glass ball on somebody and tell 'em you're sorry! What are you doing up there anyway?
Buddy. Talk to your mother.
Angel. What are they doing?
Anna. What does it look like?

Angel. Put that down.

Tony. (*cockily, sizing her up*) Any suggestions where?

Lino. Look, girlie.

Angel. Don't call me that.

Lino. All right: lady, woman, miss. A demolition order is a demolition order.

Angel. (*to ANNA*) Demolition order?

Anna. You heard the man.

Angel. (*to TONY*) I said take your hands off it. (*She has picked up a crowbar. At first, THE WRECKERS aren't sure just how serious she is.*)

Tony. Hey, c'mon, sweetheart, I just work here.

Angel. Don't mess with me. (*SLAM! ANGEL has slammed the crowbar down hard quite close to him. TONY is quite impressed.*)

Tony. Okay, okay, I hear you. (*GUY has entered.*)

Angel. Nobody's tearing this place down. This is my home. I live here. Get it?

Anna. Wrong. You used to live here. Get that. I sold the rink. It's coming down.

Angel. Sold it?

Anna. What did you expect me to do? Stay here for the rest of my life waiting for you to come back? Welcome home, Angel. What's left of it. Thanks for bringing back a lot of memories and feelings I'm gonna miss almost as much as this place. (*With a nod to THE WRECKERS:*) Gentlemen, she's all yours. (*Her gesture includes ANGEL and the rink.*)

Angel. I'm not going to let you do this.

Anna. It's already done. (*She starts up the stairs to the living quarters.*)

Angel. You come back here. I'm not through with you.

Anna. (*turning at the door*) Angel, kiss my ass.

[MUSIC CUE 8: AFTER ALL THESE YEARS]

(*She goes into the apartment, slamming the door. ANGEL is very aware of THE WRECKERS all looking at her.*)

Angel. So what are you looking at? (*brandishing the crowbar*) I'm not through with you either! (*Music. She drops the crowbar, charges up the stairs and goes into the apartment. The door is slammed. The WRECKERS look at one another.*)

THE RINK

Anna. (*offstage*) That's right, you heard me. Drop dead. (*Music. Pause. THE WRECKERS sing:*)

"AFTER ALL THESE YEARS"

Wreckers.
GEE, IT'S GOOD TO SEE YOU
AFTER ALL THESE YEARS
GEE, YOU'VE REALLY LIFTED MY MORALE
KEPT IT ALL TOGETHER
AFTER ALL THESE YEARS
WHAT'S YOUR SECRET, OLD PAL?

I CAN SEE THAT FORTUNE HAS BEEN KIND TO YOU
GUESS YOU'VE HAD NO OBSTACLES TO CLIMB

Buddy.	Others.
GEE, YOU LOOK TERRIFIC	OOH OOH
AFTER ALL THESE YEARS	OOH OOH AND

Lucky.
COMPLETELY UNCHANGED BY TIME!

Wreckers.
I CAN SEE THAT FORTUNE HAS BEEN KIND TO YOU
GUESS YOU'VE HAD NO OBSTACLES TO CLIMB . . .

(*The glitter ball flies out, and they do a little dance.*)

COMPLETELY UNCHANGED BY TIME!

I CAN SEE THAT FORTUNE HAS BEEN KIND TO YOU
GUESS YOU'VE HAD NO OBSTACLES TO CLIMB
GEE, YOU LOOK TERRIFIC
AFTER ALL THESE YEARS
COMPLETELY UNCHANGED
BY TIME!

(*ANGEL comes quickly out of the apartment and down the stairs.*)

[MUSIC CUE 9: ANGEL'S RINK AND SOCIAL CENTER]

(*She is waving a legal-looking document. ANNA is right behind her, trying to get the document back.*)

Angel. I don't believe it!

Anna. Give me that!
Angel. She forged my name!
Anna. Leave them out of this!
Angel. My own mother forged her own daughter's name!
Anna. What was I supposed to do, ask some stranger? All I did was sign her lousy name to a little piece of paper so I could unload this place. For that they're gonna give me the electric chair?
Angel. I'll settle for life imprisonment.
Anna. Quit talking like I'm a common criminal.
Angel. You are. Ma, people get twenty years for this. Grandpa left the rink to both of us.
Anna. You were a minor then.
Angel. I just grew up. And I didn't come back here to have you tell me we were going out of business. Maybe you are, Mrs. Antonelli, but I'm having a grand re-opening!
Angel.
I GOT PLANS, MA
LOTS OF PLANS
STICK AROUND, MA
WATCH 'EM HAPPEN

(*ANGEL crosses half-way up the stairs.*)

Anna. I'll tell you what's gonna happen. Nothing!
Angel.
ANGEL'S RINK AND SOCIAL CENTER
IT'S SEVEN FIFTY JUST TO ENTER
AND TWO BUCKS MORE IN CASE YOU'RE RENTING
  SKATES
AND THIS WON'T STOP ME
I WON'T LET IT
'CAUSE WE AIN'T SELLING
JUST FORGET IT
THE GOOD THINGS ALWAYS COME TO SHE WHO
  WAITS
  Guy.
HER WHO WAITS
  Angel. (*to GUY, spoken*) Ah, shut up!

Angel.	Lucky.
ANYWAY, AS I WAS SAYING	HEY, YOUR DAUGHTER'S GOT PLANS

I'M SICK OF BUSSES Lino.
SICK OF STRAYING SO DO WE GO ON?
AND SICK OF CHANGING Buddy.
  ZIP CODES THREE SO DO WE GO ON?
  TIMES A YEAR

 Men. (*variously*)
 OR DO WE GO HOME?
 OR DO WE GO HOME?
 OR DO WE GO HOME?

I'VE CLEARED MY DECKS
  AND CLEARED MY
  VISION
I MADE MYSELF A BIG
  DECISION
NOW ANGEL'S BACK
AND ANGEL'S SETTLING
HERE YOUR DAUGHTER'S GOT
   PLANS
RIGHT HERE YOUR DAUGHTER'S GOT
   PLANS
RIGHT HERE SO DO WE PACK UP?
 OR DO WE PACK IN?

  Angel. (*continued*)
I'LL BE SIPPING SOMETHING COOL
  Lucky.
HEY LADY
  Angel.
A LEMONADE, I THINK
  Men.
WHAT ABOUT IT?
  Angel.
WHILE MEDEA WILL BE COOLING HER HEELS IN THE
  CLINK
  Lino.
THAT AIN'T A WAY YOU SHOULD BE TALKING TO
  YOUR MOTHER
  Angel.
I'LL BE DINING ON A SALAD
  Guy.
ALL RIGHT
  Angel.
SO ANXIOUS TO BE THIN

Men.
HEY LADY
 Angel.
WHILE MY MOTHER WILL BE STANDING
BY SOME LADY WITH A LADLE
WHO'LL BE SLOPPING SOMETHING GLUEY
ON HER PLATE OF JAILHOUSE TIN!
 Men.
WELL, IT LOOKS AS IF WE'RE ON ANOTHER BREAK
 Angel.
AH MA
 Men.
AH MA!
 Angel.
IT COMES AS NO SURPRISE
OUR LADY OF THE LIES
HAD GUTS ENOUGH TO GO AND FORGE MY NAME
(AND BADLY)
(*spoken*) This doesn't even look like my signature.
 Anna. That's what you get for not writing more often.
 Angel & Men.
AH MA!
 Angel.
YOU SEE THAT DOTTED LINE?
THAT SIGNATURE AIN'T MINE
THIS PAPER MEANS ONE THING
YOUR ASS IS IN A SLING
(*ANGEL and ANNA are nose to nose.*)
 Men. (*pulling the women apart*)
BREAK IT UP, GIRLS
MAKE IT UP, GIRLS
 Angel.
I GOT PLANS, MA
LOTS OF PLANS
STICK AROUND, MA
WATCH 'EM HAPPEN

ANGEL'S RINK AND SOCIAL CENTER
THE CHIC-EST PLACE YOU'LL EVER ENTER
WITH BRUNCH ON SKATES SERVED EVERY SUNDAY
 AT NOON

SO YOU CAN DINE ON BELGIAN WAFFLE
OR FILL YOUR FACE ON FINE FALAFEL
A TOTAL RENOVATION'S HAPPENING SOON
REAL SOON
VERY SOON

SO THAT'S THE FUTURE, THAT'S THE STORY
I'LL HAVE THE RINK IN ALL ITS GLORY
AND I CAN MAKE IT HAPPEN, THAT MUCH I KNOW
'CAUSE NOW I'M GROWN
AND NOW I'M STRONGER
IT'S NOT THE SIXTIES ANY LONGER
I GOT THIS DREAM AND I AIN'T LETTIN' IT

                              MEN.
GO!   HEY LADY
                          DO WE SIT?
                          HEY LADY
                          DO WE SPLIT?
                          HEY LADY
                          WHAT ABOUT IT?

ANNA. Gentlemen, why don't you finish clearing out that apartment?

(*THE WRECKERS start to return to work. BUDDY opens the big door; they continue to remove the jukebox, more crates, etc.*)

ANGEL. I don't care about that stuff. It's the rink you're not touching. (*She fishes in her pocket for change.*) Can you change a half dollar?
ANNA. What for?
ANGEL. I'm calling a lawyer. (*TONY, BUDDY, GUY and BEN have exited.*)
ANNA. Get outta here. (*LUCKY and LINO cross.*)
ANGEL. I need a dime. Somebody give me a dime.
ANNA. Whoever gives her that dime is a dead person.
LINO. Leave us out of this.
ANNA. That's the first intelligent thing you've said all morning.
LUCKY. (*tossing ANGEL a dime*) Here you go.

ANGEL. Thanks. (*She runs to pay phone and dials.*)

ANNA. That's a wrap for you, sweetheart. You're a little fink. Cute. But a fink. (*He is gone, and the large door has closed behind him. To ANGEL:*) You don't know any lawyers.

ANGEL. (*indicating a name on the legal document*) Your lawyer.

ANNA. That son of a bitch! Wait'll you get his bill!

ANGEL. (*into phone*) Hello, is Mr. Maloney there?

ANNA. I'll throw myself on the mercy of the court. A bereaved widow, abandoned by her own only child . . . ! They'll never convict me.

ANGEL. (*into phone*) When do you expect him?

ANNA. Angel.

ANGEL. My name is Angela Antonelli.

ANNA. Angela! She's serious. I'm up shit creek.

ANGEL. He allowed my mother to sign some documents illegally. I want to stop the sale of the rink and I'll get a court order to do it. Have him get back to me at the rink. Yes, you can tell him it's an emergency. It's my whole damn life. (*She slams the phone down. LINO appears with a carton full of dolls and stuffed toys.*)

LINO. What about these, Mrs. A?

ANNA. (*without turning*) It all goes.

ANGEL. Those were mine!

ANNA. All of it!

LINO. You're the boss.

ANNA. Tell her that! (*LINO exits.*)

ANGEL. You're not getting away with this.

ANNA. Don't you even want to know how much I got for this place?

ANGEL. *You* got for it?

ANNA. We, we! Half of it's yours.

ANGEL. I don't want it.

ANNA. I'm talking about a lot of money.

ANGEL. Easy come, easy go.

ANNA. This is crazy. Another half hour and I would have been out that door!

ANGEL. Sorry to disappoint you. All I care about is the rink.

ANNA. All you care about is yourself.

ANGEL. Nobody else in this family ever did!

ANNA. Waiter, would you bring my little girl a cup and violin?

ANGEL. Fuck you, Ma.

ANNA. (*raising her hand to ANGEL*) Don't use that word to me. Don't you ever use it again.

ANGEL. I'm sorry. You're right. (*ANNA lowers her hand.*) Fuck you, *lady*. (*ANNA slaps her. ANGEL slaps her right back.*)

ANNA. I don't want this! (*There is a long beat.*)

ANGEL. I'm sorry. Truce?

ANNA. (*nodding; rubbing her cheek*) That hurt.

ANGEL. (*ditto*) Tell me about it.

ANNA. You're just lucky I didn't have my bridge in.

ANGEL. You know something? I can't remember you ever hitting me when I was a kid..

ANNA. No wonder you turned out the way you did. Are you pregnant?

ANGEL. No.

ANNA. You in some kind of trouble?

ANGEL. No, but you are.

ANNA. Playland's had it, Angel.

ANGEL. People have been saying that ever since I can remember.

ANNA. This time I mean it. Do you know how lucky we are to sell? Connie's Salt Water Taffy, the Levy's Bath House, the Sky Wheel—I'm talking about the original families, like your grandfather—they've all sold. They've even sold the Red Devil.

ANGEL. We just heard it.

ANNA. There wasn't anybody riding it. Mr. DiMarco runs it twice a day, empty, like he can't let go of it.

ANGEL. They can't do that. The Red Devil is Playland.

ANNA. That's what I'm talking about. It's coming down right after this place. It all is. It's not just the rink.

ANGEL. (*crossing stage* R.) We're not coming down. I don't care if we're the only place left on the boardwalk.

ANNA. It's not our boardwalk anymore.

[MUSIC CUE 10: WHAT HAPPENED TO THE OLD DAYS?]

(*Loud disco music. Lights change and the huge trusses overhead begin to move down with two other pieces of framework. When they stop, we are on the boardwalk at the foot of the rollercoaster. A large wooden tool chest that THE WRECKERS have left onstage is now a bench.*

Two PUNKS [TONY and LUCKY] appear. One of them carries a very large portable radio, which is blasting away. MRS. SILVERMAN [BEN] and MRS. JACKSON [BUDDY] appear.)

ANNA. Turn that thing down!
MRS. SILVERMAN. We can't even say "There goes the boardwalk." It's already gone.
MRS. JACKSON. It's the radios I hate the most. You know what I'm talking about?
ANGEL. The radios are everywhere. You think you're special? *(ANGEL is only an observer in this scene from ANNA's not-too-distant past.)*
ANNA. *(shaking her head)* Not like here. That's not music.
ANGEL & ANNA. *(together)* That's noise.
MRS. JACKSON. Tell me about it. *(The radio blasts again.)*
ANNA. Turn that thing down. Or I'm calling somebody!
PUNK #1. *(TONY)* Up yours, lady.
PUNK #2. *(LUCKY)* She should be so lucky.
ANNA. It's all changed, Angel. The people who came here and what they were looking for.

(The PUNKS begin to move off. ANNA sits on the tool box between the two ladies. MRS. JACKSON dusts the top before she sits down.)

MRS. JACKSON. Nice people. Good times.
ANNA. But now.
MRS. SILVERMAN. Please, don't give me now.
ANNA. They think they own the boardwalk.
ANNA, MRS. SILVERMAN, & MRS. JACKSON.
WHAT HAPPENED TO THE OLD DAYS?
ANGEL. Do I gotta hear this?
ANNA, MRS. SILVERMAN, & MRS. JACKSON.
WHAT HAPPENED TO THE OLD BOARDWALK
WHERE WE COULD PULL A CAMP CHAIR OUT
AND SIT AND CHEW THE FAT.
WHAT HAPPENED TO THE OLD DAYS
WHAT HAPPENED TO THE NEIGHBORHOOD?
ANNA.
WHY IS IT THAT YOU CAN'T GO OUT
WITHOUT A BASEBALL BAT?

ANNA, MRS. SILVERMAN & MRS. JACKSON.
WHAT'S GOING ON? WHAT'S GOING ON? WHAT'S GOING ON?
MRS. SILVERMAN. Thank God your husband didn't live to see all this. Why don't you sell like everybody else?

(*ANGEL almost comes into the scene.*)

ANNA. I promised the Antonellis I'd hang on to the rink.
ANGEL. And this Antonelli's gonna make sure you keep that promise.
ANNA. Will you listen? (*To MRS. SILVERMAN:*) Besides, maybe Angel will want to come back.
MRS. SILVERMAN. What for? Living in San Francisco with that swanky society doctor —.
MRS. JACKSON. How many grandchildren is it now?
ANNA. Five.
ANGEL. Jesus. Mama! Is that what you told people?
ANNA. I did.
MRS. SILVERMAN. My kids are trying to get me to move down to Florida with them. You know what I call it? Out of the frying pan and into the fire.
MRS. JACKSON. What's keeping you? I'd buy myself a gold lame bikini and tell 'em I was coming right on down!
MRS. SILVERMAN. I hate Florida. It's one big cemetery. This is home.
MRS. JACKSON. This *was* home, Charlotte.
ANNA. Everything is was lately.
MRS. SILVERMAN. I can remember sitting on this boardwalk late, really late. Nine, ten o'clock at night and nobody would bother you.
ANNA. Ten o'clock ain't late, Mrs. Silverman. Even in the Tenth Century, ten o'clock was never late.
MRS. SILVERMAN. Oh, well. We're just three old women now.
ANNA. What do you mean, "old?" I'm forty something.
MRS. SILVERMAN. If you don't count the something.

(*The PUNKS reappear from L. of C. with a third [LINO], who also has a radio, and with them, the deafening music. They are divvying up the contents of a woman's purse.*)

PUNK #1. How much did we get?

PUNK #2. Six lousy bucks.
PUNK #3. I told you we shoulda cut her.
ANNA. I hate what's happening here.
MRS. SILVERMAN. You're crazy to start with them, Anna.
ANGEL. She's right, Ma. Any fool knows that.
MRS. SILVERMAN. But what are we gonna do?
MRS. JACKSON. Look what they did to Mr. Lazito.
ANGEL. He runs the Bumper Cars.
ANNA. Ran! They killed him.
MRS. SILVERMAN. It's a jungle. (*ANGEL moves away.*)
ANNA & LADIES.
WHAT HAPPENED TO THE OLD DAYS?
WHAT HAPPENED TO THE EVENING STROLL
WHEN PEOPLE USED TO SAY "HELLO"
THEN GO THEIR OWN SWEET WAY

WHAT HAPPENED TO THE OLD DAYS
WHAT HAPPENED TO THE MOVIE SHOW
WHY IS IT THAT IT'S ONLY SAFE
TO SEE A MATINEE?

WHAT'S GOING ON? WHAT'S GOING ON? WHAT'S GOING ON?

MRS. JACKSON.
REMEMBER ALL THE OUT OF DOORS CONCESSIONS
WITH SILVER ON THE COUNTER?
ALL.
NOW THEY LOCK THEIR QUARTERS IN A SAFE THAT WEIGHS A TON
ANNA.
NOWADAYS YOU LOOK AT BULGING TROUSERS
LADIES.
SOME BOY WITH BULGING TROUSERS
ANNA:
IT ISN'T WHAT YOU THINK IT IS
THE BASTARD'S GOT A GUN
ALL.
IT'S MURDER

UNDER THE ROLLER COASTER
NEXT TO THE JUNGLE RIDE

RIGHT OF THE CATERPILLAR
LEFT OF THE WATER SLIDE

WHO WANTS TO BE A TARGET?
THEY SEE A PIECE OF JEWELRY
AND KNOCK YOU DOWN AND TEAR IT OFF YOUR NECK
  Mrs. Silverman.
THOSE SCUMBAGS
  All.
UNDER THE ROLLER COASTER
NEXT TO THE JUNGLE RIDE
RIGHT OF THE CATERPILLAR
LEFT OF THE WATER SLIDE

WHAT HAPPENED TO THE OLD DAYS
WHAT HAPPENED TO THE UNLOCKED DOOR
WHAT HAPPENED TO THE "COME ON IN, IT'S OPEN" KIND OF PHRASE?

WHAT HAPPENED TO THE NICE TIMES?
  Mrs. Jackson.
WHO PUT THE "HOOD" IN NEIGHBORHOOD?
  Mrs. Silverman. (*spoken*) Sell, Anna, what are you waiting for? You need a brick wall to fall on your head?

(*The PUNKS with their radios approach. ANNA starts moving toward the PUNKS.*)

Anna. Turn that thing down. I said turn that down! What are you doing here anyway?
Punk #1. Look who's here. The Mouth.
Mrs. Silverman. Don't, Anna.
Angel. You didn't, ma.
Anna. You heard me.
Punk #2. Oh, man, this is just for the asking.
Mrs. Jackson. She's crazy. (*The two ladies cross* us. *to the stairs.*)
Anna. This is ours!
Punk #3. Hey, lady, we're just trying to have a good time.
Angel. Come back, Ma.

ANNA. You've pushed us far enough. I'm saying this to you.

(*She repeats the Va Fangul gesture.*)

Music up. ANNA is stalked, cornered and mugged. ANGEL watching, horrified, powerless. The rhythm we heard from the radio turns into a stylized, yet violent/brutal dance sequence.

The PUNKS leave ANNA lying beaten. The set and lights begin to restore to "the present." MRS. SILVERMAN and MRS. JACKSON start to move off US.R.)

MRS. SILVERMAN & MRS. JACKSON.
WHAT HAPPENED TO THE OLD DAYS?
WHAT HAPPENED TO THE OLD DAYS?

ANGEL. (*crossing left to ANNA*) Always poking your nose where you shouldn't! Why didn't you tell me? I would've come and taken care of you. All you had to do was ask. But no, the big martyr. Suffer in silence.

ANNA. (*who isn't having any from her, brushing ANGEL aside, fighting back tears, wiping at her face and clothes*) Where was I supposed to find you? You're just lucky I didn't give this place away. I'm counting my blessings: some hot shot Boston developer wants to turn all this into high-rise condos, God only knows why! Can you imagine anyone coming here to retire? Living here wasn't bad enough?

ANGEL. What did you expect?

ANNA. You're not gonna queer this for me, Angel.

ANGEL. I'm not trying to, only it's not that simple.

ANNA. For once in my life I don't want to hear "No, Anna," "Don't, Anna." "You can't, Anna."

ANGEL. I know, Mama.

ANNA. I want to hear "Yes, Anna." Capisce?

ANGEL. I can't give it up, Ma. (*She picks up her duffle bag and brings it DS.C.*)

ANNA. Excuse me, I was working on a beer. (*She goes to the organ for her beer.*)

ANGEL. I gotta make another phone call. I need a dime. Please. (*ANNA tosses her a dime. ANGEL goes to phone.*) Thanks.

ANNA. I'm gonna finish packing.

[MUSIC CUE 10A: FINALE ACT I]

ANGEL. (*into phone*) Hello, this is Angela Antonelli. That's right. Thanks. (*To ANNA, who has stopped midway up the stairs:*) Do you mind? (*She waits as ANNA goes into the apartment.*) Honey, it's me. This is gonna take a little longer than I thought. I always sound funny when I'm having a terrible time. Wait for me. Yeah, the rink is beautiful. I love you, too. (*She hangs up, and crosses C. She sings:*)

BEADS AND BLEACHERS AND COLORED LIGHTS
PASSING SMILES, ROUND AND ROUND
THUMPING OOM PAH PAH ORGAN SOUND
LEAVING HOME YEARS AGO
WHAT WAS I LOOKING FOR?

(*ANNA has reappeared on the landing. ANGEL sees her.*)

WELL, ANYWAY
SOON I'LL HAVE MY DAYS AND NIGHTS
OF WONDERFUL, GLIMMERING
BEAUTIFUL, SHIMMERING
COLORED LIGHTS!

(*curtain*)

End ACT I

ACT TWO

[MUSIC CUE 10B: ENTR'ACTE]

At rise, ANNA and ANGEL are in the same positions we last saw them in. It is the next moment.

ANNA. (*coming down the stairs to* L. *of* C.) Who were you calling? Or shouldn't I ask? (*ANGEL will move* C. *to her duffle bag, take out a joint, and sit on the floor to the right of the bag.*)
ANGEL. Someone I'm traveling with.
ANNA. I shouldn't have asked. I can just see him. Long hair, needs a bath and smokes dope.
ANGEL. No, that's me. You mind if I smoke a joint?
ANNA. What if I did?
ANGEL. (*lighting up joint*) You got a point. You want a toke?
ANNA. No, thank you. What's a toke?
ANGEL. A puff, a drag; a toke!
ANNA. How do they get "toke" out of "puff?"
ANGEL. I don't know. (*She offers the joint to ANNA.*)
ANNA. You smoke this stuff and you don't even know what it means? (*ANNA smokes the joint "like a pro."*)
ANGEL. Where did you learn to do that?
ANNA. Television, (*exhales*) the soaps. (*passing the joint to ANGEL*) Where did you?
ANGEL. The girls room at Our Lady of Perpetual Sorrow Junior High. (*inhales*)
ANNA. I should've guessed.
ANGEL. (*on the exhale*) It's funny, but none of us girls turned out nuns.
ANNA. I wonder why. (*She takes the joint from ANGEL. Confidentially.*) Listen, Martha . . . Martha? . . . Angel! (*She looks at the joint, reacts.*) — before you hear it from somebody else and I'm sure you will, me and the parish are kind of on the outs the past couple of years.
ANGEL. What happened?
ANNA. They accused me of cheating at Bingo. (*ANGEL reaches for the joint, but ANNA wants another puff.*)
ANGEL. Well, did you?
ANNA. I guess.
ANGEL. (*taking the joint*) Ma! (*She inhales.*)

56

ANNA. You know how boring Bingo is? (*getting up*) Besides, it's very easy to confuse eleven with seventeen!

ANGEL. (*giving joint to ANNA and crossing* L.) Since when?

ANNA. They both go straight up and down, only the seven in seventeen has this teeny little thing going . . . (*She demonstrates with a flick of her index finger.*) . . . flick! Up top.

ANGEL. Could I see that again?

ANNA. What?

ANGEL. That teeny little line going . . . (*She imitates ANNA's gesture*) . . . flick! Up top.

ANNA. Are you making fun of me?

ANGEL. No! You're cute when you're stoned.

ANNA. (*meeting ANGEL at* C. *and giving her the joint*) I just wanted to make sure. Now where was I?

ANGEL. Cheating at Bingo.

ANNA. And you know who fingered me? (*ANNA lies down on the stage* L. *side of the duffle bag, leaning her arm on it.*)

ANGEL. (*sitting at the right end of the bag and putting out the joint*) Mrs. Carlucci?

ANNA. How did you know?

ANGEL. She's always had it in for us.

ANNA. She died six months ago. (*Long pause. They both laugh.*) You know what they sang at her funeral? Something from *Camelot*. Now you wanna talk about bad taste! It was probably the lowest moment in my life.

ANGEL. Mrs. Carlucci's funeral?

ANNA. No! Getting caught at Bingo.

[MUSIC CUE 11: THE APPLE DOESN'T FALL]

ANGEL. I got busted once.

ANNA. Yeah? What'd you do?

ANGEL. I stole a box of Easter egg dye.

ANNA. That's dumb.

ANGEL. So's Bingo.

ANNA. Why would anyone steal a box of Easter egg dye?

ANGEL. Why would anyone cheat at Bingo? What's the difference?

ANNA. Maybe we're not so different.

ANGEL. Hah!

ANNA. Think about it.

"THE APPLE DOESN'T FALL"

Angel.
I HATE UNCLE FAUSTO
Anna.
GOD, ME TOO
I HATE GROWING OLDER
Angel.
BOY, AM I WITH YOU
Anna & Angel.
SO, YOU DON'T HAVE TO BE A PROFESSOR TO SEE
THE APPLE DOESN'T FALL VERY FAR FROM THE TREE!
Angel.
I HATE DOING DISHES
ALL THAT GREASE
Anna.
I HATE MRS. CARLUCCI
MAY SHE REST IN PEACE
Anna & Angel.
THERE'S MORE THAN A FEW THINGS ON WHICH WE AGREE
THE APPLE DOESN'T FALL VERY FAR FROM THE TREE!
Anna.
FOR NINE MONTHS, I CARRIED YOU UNDER MY HEART
Angel.
AH, FOR NINE MONTHS, SELDOM IF EVER APART
Anna & Angel.
NO WONDER
Angel.
I CAN BE ANNOYING
SCREAM AND FIGHT
Anna.
SOMETIMES I'M NO LADY
Angel.
YOU GOT THAT RIGHT!
Anna & Angel.
SO, THE SAYING IS TRUE
LOOKA YOU, LOOKA ME
THE APPLE DOESN'T FALL VERY FAR —
FROM THE TREE!

(*TONY and BUDDY enter from the apartment, each carrying a chair, and come down the stairs. ANGEL and ANNA turn* US., *leaning on their elbows, to look.*)

TONY. You two okay?
ANNA. We're fabulous. Come on down! (*She waves to the men to join them on the floor.*)
BUDDY. Catch you ladies later.

(*BUDDY takes both chairs and exits* R. *TONY turns, puts his foot on the stairs, and bends over to tie his shoe. He suddenly realizes that the two ladies are looking at his backside, and exits.*

ANNA and ANGEL turn front on the bag, look at each other a long time, and finally burst into laughter.)

ANGEL.
ME. I LIKE TO STROKE SOME BIG GUY'S CHEST
ANNA.
SPECIALLY ITALIANS
ANNA & ANGEL.
HONEY
THEY'RE THE BEST
YOU DON'T NEED A SHEEPSKIN FROM HARVARD TO SEE
THE APPLE DOESN'T FALL VERY FAR FROM THE TREE
ANNA.
ME, I LIKE A GUY WHO'LL SCRATCH MY BACK
ANGEL.
TRY A LITTLE LOWER
ANNA. (*in a very low voice*)
SCRATCH MY BACK
ANNA & ANGEL (*laughing*)
IT'S SWEET WHEN A MOTHER AND DAUGHTER AGREE
THE APPLE DOESN'T FALL VERY FAR FROM THE TREE
ANGEL. (*rolling over onto her back*)
FOR NINE MONTHS, AT LEAST I WAS NEVER IGNORED
ANNA.
AH, FOR NINE MONTHS, I GAVE YOU FREE ROOM AND BOARD
ANGEL. (*turning back onto her stomach*)
YOU'RE TOPS, MA

ANNA.
I KNOW I SHOULDN'T SAY THIS
ANGEL.
BE MY GUEST
ANNA.
WE'RE NOT SO VERY DIFFERENT
ANGEL.
NOW, I'M REAL DEPRESSED
WELL, YOU OPEN A TEA BAG, THERE'S GONNA BE TEA

(*She moves behind ANNA, reaching left for the beercan.*)

ANNA. (*leaning DS.R., opposite to ANGEL*)
YOU OPEN A PEA POD AND GUESS WHAT? A PEA
ANNA & ANGEL.
AND THE APPLE DOESN'T FALL VERY FAR
FROM THE TREE!

(*During the applause, ANNA reaches to touch ANGEL's hair; ANGEL pulls away.*)

ANNA. It's nice to see you, Angel.

ANGEL. We're just stoned.

ANNA. No, I mean it. I . . . (*The moment slips away almost as quickly as it happened.*)

ANGEL. I can be had, ma, but not that easy. (*getting up*) Excuse me. (*She crosses US. with the duffle and places it under the stairs.*)

ANNA. Forget it.

ANGEL. (*crossing down C. to ANNA's right*) Some mothers would consider themselves lucky to have a daughter to carry on the family tradition.

ANNA. This isn't a tradition. It's a dump.

ANGEL. Put it on a postcard.

ANNA. Oh I will! (*She's up.*) All the way from Rome!

ANGEL. Rome? (*crossing DS.R.*) You mean, over there Rome?

ANNA. I'm taking a little vacation. I never had one, Miss Global Trot.

ANGEL. (*crossing C. to ANNA*) You going with someone? Or shouldn't I ask? (*no reply*) I shouldn't have asked.

ANNA. I'm going with Lenny.

[MUSIC CUE 12: MARRY ME]

ANGEL. Who's Lenny?

ANNA. You remember good old Lenny . . .

(*Lights change. LENNY appears US. walking slowly towards ANNA and ANGEL.*)

LENNY. (*singing*)
GOOD OLD LENNY
ANNA. Sure you do. Good old Lenny Pegedis. He owned the moon rockets. (*She moves to the bar.*)
LENNY.
GOOD OLD, GOOD OLD LENNY
(*LENNY moves to the bar and sits next to ANNA.*)

THEY NEVER CALL ME LENNY
OR LEONARD OR LEN
IT'S ALWAYS GOOD OLD LENNY
GOOD OLD, GOOD OLD LENNY
SINCE I CAN'T REMEMBER WHEN

(*ANNA and ANGEL are both a little high now.*)

ANGEL. He's been after you since I was that high.
ANNA. He's been after me since *I* was that high!

(*ANNA swings around on her stool and takes a coke with a straw from behind the bar. She is now a young girl. ANGEL crosses US. behind the bar and leans on the DS. edge of the bar to watch this scene from the past.*)

LENNY.
GOOD OLD LENNY . . .
GOOD OLD, GOOD OLD, GOOD OLD LENNY
THEY ONLY SEEM TO KNOW ME THAT WAY
BUT GOOD OLD LENNY
GOOD OLD, GOOD OLD LENNY
HAS SOMETHING IMPORTANT TO SAY:

"MARRY ME"

MARRY ME
COME ON AND MARRY ME
WHY NOT AGREE TO BE
MY BLUSHING BRIDE?

I KNOW THE NEIGHBORHOOD
WOULD GIVE ITS CONSENT
AND THERE'S A CUTAWAY
I'M DYING TO RENT

(*ANNA has been playing with his tie. As he touches her left hand she pulls it away.*)

THE DAY YOU
MARRY ME
GIVE IN AND MARRY ME
I REALLY LOVE YOU, SEE?
WE CAN'T GO WRONG

THAT DIAMOND IN THE STORE
I COULD PAY MONTHLY FOR
COME ON AND MARRY ME,
MARRY ME, MARRY ME

(*She turns away on the stool — LENNY turns her back to him.*)

ANNA. (*as a young girl*) I'm too young. Besides, I'm never going to marry a boy from the park.
ANGEL. (*in the present*) Famous last words.
LENNY. What about that Dino Antonelli?
ANNA. What about him?
LENNY. He likes you.
ANNA. What girl doesn't he like, that Dino Antonelli? He's a conceited, stuck up moron. Just because his family owns the skating rink, they think they're something special.
LENNY. If you ever change your mind, I'll be here. (*He kisses her and begins to back* US.) I'm no Dino Antonelli, Anna, I'm just Lenny Pegedis but I love you. (*sings:*)
SO, MARRY ME
GIVE IN AND MARRY ME
THOUGH YOU DON'T LOVE ME NOW
YOU WILL IN TIME

YOU MAY NOT KNOW IT YET
BUT I'M THE BEST YOU'LL GET
WAKE UP AND MARRY ME
ANNA. Lenny . . .

LENNY.
MARRY ME
  ANGEL. He sure was sweet, Ma.
  ANNA. Good old Lenny . . .
LENNY.
MARRY ME

   [MUSIC CUE 12A: ARNIE'S UNDERSCORE]

(*He is gone. ARNIE [LUCKY], a contemporary of the young ANNA and LENNY, comes running in with CHARLIE [BUDDY], another pal. ANGEL crosses* US.R. *to watch.*)

  ARNIE. Hey, Anna! I got two tickets for the Red Sox game. What do ya say?
  ANNA. Hi, Arnie.
  CHARLIE. Forget it, Arnie.
  ARNIE. How about it?
  ANNA. I'm sorry, Arnie, I'm going with . . .
  ARNIE & CHARLIE. (*sing song*) Dino Antonelli!

(*CHARLIE takes ARNIE out the right door ad libbing as DINO appears at the* US.L. *gate with a case of coke bottles, which he carries behind the bar.*)

  ANGEL. (*crossing back to ANNA*) You were popular!
  ANNA. You don't have to say it like that!
  ANGEL. No, it's funny to imagine you that age.
  ANNA. Even then, I only had eyes for your father. (*DINO kisses ANNA. His hands are all over her. He is very persistent.*) I love you, Dino.
  DINO. I love you, too. (*DINO's FATHER and his UNCLE FAUSTO [LINO] have appeared at the* US.L. *gate.*)
  UNCLE FAUSTO. Love!
  DINO. It's my uncle. Don't let him see you. (*He gently pushes ANNA to the floor and sits next to her.*)
  UNCLE FAUSTO. What kind of love at their age. He's got a hard on and she will not put out.
  DINO's FATHER. Shut up, Fausto. Just because she won't have nothing to do with you.
  ANNA. (*to ANGEL*) Your Uncle Fausto.
  ANGEL. I never liked him.

ANNA. You had good taste.
UNCLE FAUSTO. He'll be marrying beneath us.
ANNA. (*to ANGEL*) Can you imagine beneath *that*? The mind boggles.

(*DINO takes ANNA's hand. DINO's FATHER goes to the snack bar for a bromo, then he and UNCLE FAUSTO will cross up the stairs.*)

UNCLE FAUSTO. Her people are vendors. They sell from carts.
DINO'S FATHER. I like this Anna. My son likes this Anna. That's good enough for me.
ANNA. (*to ANGEL*) The only Antonelli I really liked.
ANGEL. Gramps? Me, too.
DINO. Goodnight, Pop.
UNCLE FAUSTO. (*exiting into the apartment*) She's trash. Her people are trash.
DINO'S FATHER. (*at the top of the stairs*) Shut up, Fausto. Dino, turn off the lights before you come up.

(*They are gone. DINO is persisting with ANNA.*)

DINO. Come on, Anna, let me.
ANNA. Don't, Dino. Sister says we can't. It's a sin.
DINO. I love you, Anna! (*He chases her through the left gate, around the US. gate, and back to C. stage.*)
ANNA. When we're married. Not before.
DINO. Please.
ANNA. No, I said.

(*As he goes out the US. left gate, the lights change, the musical underscoring halts, and it is "the present" for a moment. ANNA continues to ANGEL.*)

ANNA. (*continued*) Your old lady was a virgin when she got married.
ANGEL. (*skeptical*) If you say so.
ANNA. (*It's important to her.*) I do!
ANGEL. Okay, okay!

(*Light change. We hear church organ weddiing music. A wedding party assembles around ANNA and DINO as DINO's FATHER and UNCLE FAUSTO have appeared at the top of the stairs. They join the procession as they speak to each other.)*

UNCLE FAUSTO. I don't care if Dino swears she's still got her cherry, trash is trash.
DINO'S FATHER. What do you care, Fausto?
UNCLE FAUSTO. (*crossing* DS.) The family honor is at stake.

(*DINO has come from the* US. *left gate, with ARNIE, CHARLIE, and another friend [TONY] in formal dress. ANGEL has moved to ANNA's right.*)

ANNA. What a pig!
ANGEL. You don't know!
ANNA. I know. I lived with it. What do you mean, I don't know?
UNCLE FAUSTO. She don't want Dino. She just wants the rink.
DINO'S FATHER. Basta!
ANNA. I got your rink. I've had your rink! Up to here!
DINO'S FATHER. All I want to know: is she a good worker, Dino? (*He is straightening DINO's tie.*)
DINO. Papa, would I marry a woman who wasn't a good everything? How do I look?

(*During ANNA's next speech, everyone is assembling in front of the organ to pose for wedding photographs.*)

ANNA. (*to ANGEL*) Forget "woman." Forget "good." Forget "everything." "Worker" was the only word when you married an Antonelli. How do I look?
ANGEL. (*softly*) Beautiful. (*They all pose together. There is a flash.*)
ANNA. The day your father handed me a broom was the day I should've guessed what being married to him was gonna be like. (*pose and flash*) Did I ever tell you about our honeymoon? (*pose and flash*) A weekend in Atlantic City . . . (*pose and flash*) . . . to see how his cousins ran their rink.

(*Pose, flash, and the wedding party is moving off* US.L. *as lights change, leaving ANNA and ANGEL in "the present."*)

ANGEL. That's all you remember about your honeymoon?
ANNA. Oh no, oh no!

ANGEL. I didn't think so.

ANNA. Your father and I . . . we . . . you don't want to hear this!

ANGEL. (*sitting with ANNA on the organ bench*) You're blushing.

ANNA. That part was good.

ANGEL. How good?

ANNA. Real good. The trouble was, after a while it wasn't enough.

[MUSIC CUE 12B: BLUE CRYSTAL/KOREA]

(*Lights change abruptly to 1956. DINO appears US.L., furious.*)

DINO. I said lay off me, Anna.

ANNA. (*crossing C. to DINO*) You see this tongue? Look at it. Rip it out of my mouth. That's the only way you're gonna shut me up. (*ANGEL rises and pushes the bench under the organ.*)

DINO. Not in front of the kid.

ANNA. (*to ANGEL*) Go to your room! (*ANGEL doesn't move.*)

DINO. I'm dying here, Anna. Something's wrong.

ANNA. You've been saying that ever since you came back. They shoot you in the brain over there?

DINO. You're making me wish they had. (*The music fades.*)

ANNA. Dino, I'm sorry. I'm trying to understand.

DINO. It's simple. I'm going crazy.

ANGEL. Don't fight.

ANNA. I said go to your room. (*ANGEL moves to the stairs. To DINO:*) You want to sell the rink? We'll do it — (*She snaps her fingers.*) It's gone!

DINO. Now you're the one who's talking crazy. The rink is all we got.

ANNA. I'm talking dreams, Dino. What's crazy about a dream?

DINO. They don't come true.

ANGEL & ANNA. Don't say that.

ANNA. Will you get up there! She's always listening to us. (*ANGEL clambers up into the apartment.*) Dino, we got our whole life ahead of us.

DINO. What life? Bingo tonight at Our Lady's. Bingo tomorrow night at Our Lady's. Two skating sessions seven days a week. Open the rink, close the rink. Eat, screw, fart. More kids.

More payments. More, more, more. That's our life.

(*ANGEL is having a nightmare.*)

ANGEL. (*from offstage*) Papa!
ANNA. What about her?
DINO. Don't let her hate me.
ANNA. Don't put that on me. That's not up to me.

(*DINO's FATHER has entered from the center gate, and crosses* DS. *to DINO.*)

DINO'S FATHER. If you do this, if you leave this woman, your daughter, my granddaughter, to follow that thing you got between your legs, then you're even crazier than I thought you was and that's pretty goddamn crazy.
DINO. Papa!
DINO'S FATHER. *Silenzio!* I came to this country with nothing. With sweat, with guts, with every inch of me I built all this — for you. Something for the future, 'cause you weren't even born yet. And now you have the *cugliones* to tell me you don't want this? You don't want my whole life?
DINO. I don't know what I want.
ANGEL. (*from offstage*) Papa!
ANNA. Give us another month, Dino!
DINO. What'd be the point?
ANNA. What'd be the point!
DINO'S FATHER. (*crossing up the stairs*) I give you the rink, Anna. You and Angel.
ANNA. I don't want the rink. I want Dino.
DINO'S FATHER. I tell you this, *figlio mio*: you're dead to me. You don't exist. (*crosses himself*) I have no son.

[MUSIC CUE 13: WE CAN MAKE IT (REPRISE)]

(*He goes. DINO is packed and ready to go.*)

DINO. I'm sorry, Anna. I'm honest to God sorry.
ANNA. Then don't do this to me.
DINO. I can't help it.
ANNA. I'll die if you leave me, Dino.
DINO. I'll die if I stay here.
ANNA. I will die. You don't know me. (*She reaches for him, he pulls away.*)

DINO. We don't know one another.

(*He goes out the right door. Thunder, lightning. Lights change and time jumps ahead a bit. ANGEL runs on from the apartment.*)

ANGEL. Papa!
ANNA. (*sitting on the steps*) Here I am, Angel. It's only a dream.
ANGEL. I want Papa!
ANNA. Don't, honey. Now you gotta stop this. You know he's dead.
ANGEL. I don't like dead. Dead is bad.
ANNA. (*hugging her fiercely*) Just don't you leave me, Angel. (*ANGEL sits next to her.*)

"WE CAN MAKE IT" (REPRISE)

ANNA. (*holding ANGEL*)
PEOPLE MAY HURT US
WE CAN TAKE IT
HERE COMES A BAD DAY
WE CAN SHAKE IT
I HAVE YOU, YOU HAVE ME
WE CAN MAKE IT

RIGHT TO THE END OF ALWAYS
DOWN TO THE FINISH LINE
WE CAN MAKE IT
FINE!

[MUSIC CUE 13A: QUINTET PART I]

(*THREE MEN [TONY, BUDDY, and LUCKY] appear* US.L. *in a spotlight.*)

FIRST MAN.
ANNA
ANNA.
NOT TONIGHT
SECOND MAN.
COME ON

ANNA.
GO AWAY
THIRD MAN.
YOU KNOW YOU WANT IT
ANNA.
I'M WITH MY KID
THIRD MAN.
I'LL WAIT

(*ANGEL is still in her mother's arms.*)

ANGEL. Don't worry, mama. Papa's in Purgatory. Sister Philomena says that's where men like him go before God lets them into the Kingdom of Heaven.
ANNA. She's got a lot to say for herself for a nun! Now, lights out. I gotta go.
ANGEL. Is it a sin not to be pretty, Ma?
ANNA. Who put that idea in your head? That damn nun?
ANGEL. No one, Ma. Good night.
ANNA. Good night, Angel. (*She moves away from ANGEL.*)
ALL THREE. (*crossing* DS.)
HEY MRS. A
MRS. A
HEY MRS. A
DON'T KEEP ME WAITING
ANNA.
GO TO HELL
ALL THREE.
HEY MRS. A
MRS. A
HEY MRS. A
YOU KNOW YOU WANT IT
ANNA, ANNA, ANNA, ANNA

(*Lights change—a spotlight comes up* DS. *ANNA walks into the light, crosses herself and kneels. A PRIEST [GUY] in black vestments appears.*)

ANNA. Bless me, Father, for I have sinned. It's been . . . not long enough since my last confession, Father. You gotta help me. I'm having trouble being alone, Father. Alone as a woman, you know?

PRIEST. It's His will, Mrs. Antonelli.

ANNA. I'm not talking about His will. I'm talking about my feelings.

PRIEST. For your penance, say a Rosary and ask Him for guidance. (*He disappears.*)

ANNA. You say a Rosary. And tell Him I don't like His rules.

THREE MEN.
HEY MRS. A
MRS. A
YOU KNOW YOU WANT IT
MRS. A
I'M WAITING FOR YOU

MAN #1. (*BUDDY, spoken*) Hey, Frankie. Did you ever get close to that?

MAN #2 *(TONY) Did* I?
SOMEDAY I'M GONNA TELL YOU ABOUT THE NIGHTS
SOMEDAY I'M GONNA TELL YOU ABOUT THE NIGHTS
(*THE MEN return* US.)

ANNA. (*still on her knees; lifts head to God*)
LISTEN YOU
I DON'T WANT TO WAKE UP TOMORROW
WHAT DO YOU THINK OF THAT?
I KNOW HOW I'LL WAKE UP TOMORROW
A BITTER, ANGRY LADY GETTING OLD
LISTEN YOU
IT'S HARD GETTING THROUGH THE MORNING
IT'S WORSE GETTING THROUGH THE DAY
AND I HAVEN'T EVEN STARTED ABOUT THE NIGHTS
SOME DAY I'M GONNA TELL YOU ABOUT THE NIGHTS
SOME DAY I'M GONNA TELL YOU ABOUT THE NIGHTS
I GOT A FEELING YOU DON'T KNOW ABOUT 'EM, HELL,
I GOT A FEELIN YOU DON'T KNOW ABOUT A LOT OF
  THINGS
LIKE THE NIGHTS
LISTEN YOU
I DON'T WANT TO WAKE UP TOMORROW
BITTER, ANGRY, OLD (*rising*)
NOT CARING IF I LIVE THROUGH ANOTHER DAY . . .
  OR ANOTHER NIGHT
THAT'S A LOUSY WAY TO FEEL
AND IT MAKES ME MAD

THE RINK

THAT'S RIGHT . . . I'M MAD AT YOU . . . IT TURNS ME
  AGAINST YOU
THAT'S RIGHT
I'M TURNING AGAINST YOU
THAT'S RIGHT
WHAT KIND OF A GOD ARE YOU ANYWAY?
I GUESS YOU'RE NOT REALLY THERE
YOU'RE NOT REALLY THERE
I DON'T BELIEVE
I DON'T BELIEVE IN YOU
I DON'T BELIEVE IN YOU
I DON'T BELIEVE IN YOU (*She kneels again.*)
IN THE NAME OF THE FATHER AND THE SON AND
  THE HOLY GHOST.
AMEN.

(*Light change. ANNA is preparing to go out. She crosses near the stairs, powdering her nose. A pubescent ANGEL, on the stairs, has lit a cigarette.*)

ANGEL. So where are you going tonight?
ANNA. Bingo.
ANGEL. You played Bingo last night.
ANNA. I like Bingo. Don't you have homework?
ANGEL. Yes, Ma. What if Lenny calls?
ANNA. Tell him I'm out.
ANGEL. I'll tell him you're at the hospital rolling bandages.
ANNA. You're getting too old for this. You should know better.
ANGEL. Yes, Ma.
ANNA. Don't "Yes, Ma" me all the time.
ANGEL. Yes, Ma.
ANNA. And put out that cigarette. You're too young to smoke.
ANGEL. (*putting out the cigarette*) I'm thirteen. I'm grown up.
ANNA. You're twelve and I'll tell you when you're grown up. Listen, there's hope for you yet. Lose a couple of pounds, fix your hair . . . (*at a reaction from ANGEL*) Hey, I'm kidding! Where's your sense of humor? That's one thing you *did* get from me. Use it! Give Mama a kiss. How do I look?
ANGEL. Beautiful.

(*ANGEL moves to the top of the stairs. The THREE MEN move* DS.C. *ANNA crosses down* L. *to the MEN.*)

[OPTIONAL CUT:

   THREE MEN.
HEY MRS. A
MRS. A
   ANNA. (*spoken*) I'm too young to have this happen to me.]

   THREE MEN.
COME ON, ANNA
YOU KNOW YOU WANT IT
COME ON, ANNA
I'M WAITING FOR YOU
   ANGEL.
I HEARD YOU
I HEARD YOU
REMEMBER THE WALLS WERE LIKE TISSUE PAPER
(*THE MEN are fondling ANNA. She moans.*)
   THREE MEN.
COME ON, ANNA
I'M WAITING FOR YOU
(*A light comes up on LENNY.*)
   LENNY. (*appearing from the curtain at the snack bar*)
COME ON AND MARRY ME
YOU KNOW I'LL WAIT FOR YOU
MY WHOLE LIFE LONG
(*He is gone.*)
   ANGEL.
HEARING SOUNDS
MYSTERIOUS FAMILIAR SOUNDS
AND I WOULD LIE THERE PICTURING
THE SCENE BEHIND THE DOOR
SOME STRANGER'S WHISPERS
THE BEDSPRINGS CREAKING
AND HOW MY MOTHER CAME TO MAKE THEM ALL
FAMILIAR SOUNDS
   THREE MEN. (*moving us. to the rail*)
HEY MRS. A
MRS. A
HEY MRS. A

ANGEL. (*from the c. of the platform*)	ANNA. (*right of c. stage*)	3 MEN. (*cont'd.*)
	SOMEDAY I'M	

THE RINK

MY FATHER WOULD COME INTO MY ROOM	GONNA TELL YOU ABOUT THE NIGHTS	
AND HE WOULD HOLD ME	SOMEDAY I'M GONNA TELL YOU ABOUT THE NIGHTS	
AND HE WOULD SING TO ME	YOU LIE THERE CRYING	MRS. A!
AND MAKE THE GHOSTS GO AWAY	THERE'S NO ONE BESIDE YOU	MRS. A!
MY FATHER WOULD ALWAYS UNDERSTAND	THE BED IS EMPTY THE WALLS ARE LAUGHING AT YOU	MRS. A! MRS. A! MRS. A!
SOMEDAY I'M GONNA TELL YOU ABOUT THE NIGHTS	SOMEDAY I'M GONNA TELL YOU ABOUT THE NIGHTS	
SOMEDAY WHEN I BELIEVE I CAN TALK TO YOU WHEN I AM OLD ENOUGH	SOMEDAY YOU'LL UNDERSTAND ALL ABOUT THE NIGHTS AND YOU'LL FORGIVE ME YOU'LL UNDERSTAND IT	MRS. A!
WHEN YOU'LL LISTEN WHY I LOVED HIM SO HOW I HATED THE OTHERS	YOU'LL BE A WOMAN AND YOU WON'T BLAME ME	

AND YOU
MOST OF ALL!　　　ANYMORE!
　Three Men. (*cont'd.*)
HEY MRS. A
DON'T KEEP ME WAITING!
HEY MRS. A
YOU KNOW YOU WANT IT!
HEY MRS. A
I'M WAITING FOR YOU!
ANNA! ANNA! ANNA! ANNA!

(*On applause, THE MEN exit* L. *as the light changes. ANNA and ANGEL are alone in "The present." ANGEL comes down the stairs.*)

　Anna. I was a young woman. What did you expect me to do?
　Angel. You were my mother. I expected you to love me.
　Anna. I did love you.
　Angel. Not enough.
　Anna. Then you should've been more lovable. (*ANNA realizes she's gone too far.*)
　Angel. Do what you want but I'm keeping the rink.
　Anna. We're not talking about the rink!
　Angel. Yes we are! I suddenly have a yen for some salt water taffy. (*She moves towards the small right door.*)
　Anna. Don't you walk away from this.
　Angel. What is it you used to say? "Poof! I'm invisible."
　Anna. Come back here. We're not finished.
　Angel. I wouldn't count on it. (*to LINO, who is entering from the right door with BEN*) You so much as touch one brick, I'll have you all in court so fast your heads will spin. (*ANGEL exits onto boardwalk. ANNA stands looking after her.*)
　Lino. The daughter! I knew this was gonna happen. Hey, Mrs. A, when are you two gonna settle things?
　Anna. (*starting up the stairs*) They *are* settled. She just gets a little emotional.
　Ben. I don't blame her. It's a shame to see a place like this come down.
　Lino. Do me a favor: don't tell her that. (*ANNA exits into the apartment.*)
　Ben. This place survived the hurricane of thirty-seven. It sur-

THE RINK

vived the big fire in 1950. The only thing it's not gonna survive is us.

LINO. Ha! The old philosopher! What got into you?

BEN. They're never gonna build something like this again.

(*From nowhere, a skate suddenly whizzes past their feet.*)

[MUSIC CUE 14: THE RINK]

BEN. Even if they wanted to, they wouldn't know how. After this place is gone, there's no more where it came from.

(*From somewhere else comes another skate, with a third on its trail, chasing it across the stage. Laughter is heard from unseen WRECKERS, who all come on with skates that they've found.*)

GUY. Are we on a break?

LINO. Your whole life is a break. All right, all right. Take five.

(*They all begin to put on skates. BEN continues.*)

BEN. High rises are a dime a dozen!

LINO. So were rinks. I can remember when every burg on the Eastern seaboard had one.

BEN. I can remember when every burg on the Eastern seaboard had several.

"THE RINK"

BEN.
I PLANNED ON TAKING POLLY TO THE PICTURE SHOW
BUT WHEN I CAME TO CALL, SHE SHOOK HER HEAD
SHE TOLD ME, "I GET NERVOUS AT THE PICTURE SHOW
HERE IS WHERE I'D RATHER GO INSTEAD:

"I WANNA GO 'ROUND THE RINK, THE RINK
THERE'S NOTHING TO BEAT THE RINK, I THINK
IF I'M GONNA GO AROUND WITH YOU
I WANNA GO 'ROUND THE RINK

"I WANNA GO SEE THE SPOT GO PINK
I WANNA GO HEAR THE SKATE KEY CLINK

IF YOU WANNA GOOD GO ROUND WITH ME
WE'RE GONNA GO 'ROUND THE RINK"

   LINO.
I MADE A DATE WITH SUE TO HEAR SINATRA SING
SHE SNEERED AND TOLD ME, "FRANK SINATRA, YUK!
IT'S JUST A WASTE OF CASH TO HEAR SINATRA SING
BUT TELL ME, HAVE YOU GOT A HALF A BUCK?

"BECAUSE I
WANNA GO ROUND THE RINK, THE RINK
THERE'S NOTHING TO BEAT THE RINK, I THINK
IF I'M GONNA GO AROUND WITH YOU
I WANNA GO ROUND THE RINK
   LINO & BEN.
"I WANNA GO SEE THE SPOT GO PINK
I WANNA GO HEAR THE SKATE KEY CLINK
IF YOU WANNA GOOD GO ROUND WITH ME
WE'RE GONNA GO ROUND THE RINK"
   BUDDY.
AT LAST I LEARNED TO GIVE THE LADIES WHAT
   THEY WANT
AND FURTHERMORE NOT THROW MY DOUGH AWAY
   GUY.
I NEVER TAKE THEM TO A FANCY RESTAURANT
I CALL THEM UP AND THIS IS WHAT I SAY
"MY DEAR
   ALL.
"WE'RE GONNA GO ROUND THE RINK, THE RINK
THERE'S NOTHING TO BEAT THE RINK, I THINK
IF I'M GONNA GO AROUND WITH YOU
WE'RE GONNA GO ROUND THE RINK

"WE'RE GONNA GO SEE THE SPOT GO PINK
WE'RE GONNA GO HEAR THE SKATE KEY CLINK
IF YOU WANNA GOOD GO ROUND WITH ME
WE'RE GONNA GO ROUND THE RINK"

(*The two refrains above are sung as rounds, first in three parts,*
   then in six; then, in unison:)

   ALL.
"WE'RE GONNA GO ROUND THE RINK, THE RINK
THERE'S NOTHING TO BEAT THE RINK, I THINK

IF I'M GONNA GO AROUND WITH YOU
WE'RE GONNA GO ROUND THE RINK

"WE'RE GONNA GO SEE THE SPOT GO PINK
WE'RE GONNA GO HEAR THE SKATE KEY CLINK
IF YOU WANNA GOOD GO ROUND WITH ME
IF YOU WANNA GAIN SOME GROUND WITH ME

  BEN. (*slowly, for the big finish*)
"PURE HAPPINESS CAN BE FOUND WITH ME
  ALL. (*gathering speed*)
"BY GOING AROUND
BY GOING AROUND
BY GOING AROUND AND ROUND AND ROUND
AND ROUND AND ROUND AND ROUND AND ROUND
AND ROUND AND ROUND AND ROUND AND ROUND
AND ROUND
THE RINK!"

(*The phone is ringing.*)

  LUCKY. Isn't somebody gonna get that?
  LINO. Stay out of it, Lucky. Come on, move it! (*WRECKERS begin to move off. LUCKY goes to rink door and calls off to ANGEL on the boardwalk.*)
  LUCKY. Hey!

(*He waves her inside. All THE WRECKERS save LUCKY are gone as ANGEL comes racing back in.*)

  LUCKY. The phone! Hurry up!
  ANGEL. (*running* DS.R. *to the phone*) Thanks! (*She answers phone.*) Hello.

(*ANNA has appeared on the landing with two suitcases.*)

  ANNA. You and that damn dime. (*She comes down the stairs. LUCKY is taking off his skates.*)
  ANGEL. It's for you.
  ANNA. He's your lawyer now.
  ANGEL. It's Lenny.
  ANNA. Well why didn't you say so? (*She drops her bags and runs to the phone.*) Lenny? Is something wrong? (*to ANGEL*) Do you mind?

ANGEL. Just make it quick. (*ANGEL moves away from the phone area and* US.C.)

LUCKY. (*crossing right to ANGEL*) I thought it might be that lawyer.

ANGEL. Thanks.

LUCKY. (*on his way out*) Hang in there. It's the same with me and my father.

ANGEL. What, you own a rink and your father's running off to Italy with his high school sweetheart? (*LUCKY goes out the US.L. gate. ANGEL leans on the bottom of the stair railing.*)

ANNA. (*on the phone, her purse open*) My passport's right here. I'm holding it, Lenny. It's in my hand. *And* the tickets. (*ANGEL just stares at ANNA.*) I'll be out front. Hurry up. I love you, too. (*She hangs up. She looks across at ANGEL. There is a flustered pause.*) Lenny's a worrier. If you ever see someone parked in a brown Toyota with his seat belt on, that's Lenny.

ANGEL. *Do* you love him?

ANNA. Lenny likes me. There's not too many people I can say that about right now. Yeah, I love him. You wanna see me turn a cartwheel? (*She goes for her luggage.*)

ANGEL. You gonna marry him?

ANNA. People our age don't get married. We set up light housekeeping and wait for our social security checks. How do I look?

ANGEL. Beautiful. Just go. This is all up to lawyers now. You've never been here for me anyway.

ANNA. What are you talking about?

ANGEL. I was never good enough for you. You never once told me I was pretty.

ANNA. You were pretty.

ANGEL. You were prettier.

ANNA. It wasn't a contest.

ANGEL. You made it feel like one.

ANNA. This is crazy.

ANGEL. Don't worry, Ma. You won. You always won.

[MUSIC CUE 15: WALLFLOWER PART I]

(*Light transition. We are going back to 1965 when ANGEL was a senior in high school. We will be in her bedroom as she prepares for the spring prom. ANNA will be fussing over her. ANGEL looks in an imaginary mirror and groans.*)

ANNA. (*crossing behind the bar*) There you go again. Putting yourself down.

ANGEL. It's self-defense. Before *you* do. Look at me!

ANNA. You look at you! You are going to the Our Lady of Perpetual Sorrow Senior Class Spring Prom—of which I just happen to be the parental coordinator and whose theme for this year: A Night in Honolulu was *my* idea; I've had April in Paris up to here—if I have to drag you there myself. (*She crosses to ANGEL with two lei.*)

ANGEL. I hate this dress.

ANNA. It's beautiful. I wore it to Hampshire Beach two years ago and got a lot of whistles.

ANGEL. I don't want whistles.

ANNA. Every woman wants whistles. They just don't know how to get 'em.

ANGEL. I don't have a date, Ma.

ANNA. You don't need a date. It's your house. Why do you think I donated the rink? Born yesterday this one was not! (*She has finished dressing ANGEL.*) Turn around. (*ANNA puts tissue in each side of ANGEL's brassiere.*) Now put these in there.

ANGEL. (*Taking out the tissues, she crosses to the bar and sits. With sarcasm:*) Sister Philomena says that's a sin.

ANNA. Honey, if you're gonna listen to a Catholic nun about things like that you're gonna get real screwed up. I'll tell you what's a sin. Having a party in your own house and not having a good time. Now that's a sin.

"WALLFLOWER"

ANNA. (*crossing R.*)
NEVER BE A
WALLFLOWER
SITTING ON A CHAIR
UP AGAINST THE WALL
WAITING FOR SOME BOY TO SAY,
"WOULD YOU CARE TO DANCE?"
(*sitting next to ANGEL*)

NEVER TAKE A CHANCE ON IT
NEVER EVEN ONCE
MUSTN'T BE THE DUNCE
WAITING FOR THE LOOK AND
"HEY, HOW ABOUT A TWIRL?"
NOT MY LITTLE GIRL!

(*She takes ANGEL's hand and brings her* c. *stage.*)

YOU'VE GOT TO STAND, BABY
TALL AND PROUD
GET NOTICED BY THE CROWD

MOVE, BABY
MAKE YOUR BID
AND YOU CAN HEAT IT UP THE WAY YOUR MOMMA DID

WHO WANTS A
WALLFLOWER
WILTING IN THE NIGHT
HANDS ACROSS YOUR LAP
NOT HAVING ANY FUN AT ALL
PLASTERED TO THE WALL
(*music under*)

ANNA. (*continued*) Now who's your favorite boy in the whole senior class?

ANGEL. I don't have one.

ANNA. I could think of twenty. (*ANGEL mumbles a name.*) Who?

ANGEL. Bobby Perillo.

ANNA. (*mock swaying of the knees*) Bobby Perillo! I could go for him myself. You see the ass on that kid?

ANGEL. Ma!

ANNA. Kidding. But did you? (*ANNA laughs but ANGEL is a tough house to play to.*) Now this is what we're gonna do. You're gonna walk right up to him, like this, watch me! Smile right at him and say, "Hey, Bobby Perillo, you wanna dance?" That's what they call the direct approach. It couldn't be easier. Now go on, you try it. I'll be Bobby Perillo. You be you. (*The music stops. ANGEL is speechless.*) Speak, Angel. Say something. Talk to us. (*nothing*) "Dance, Angel?" "Gee, Bobby, I'd love to."

THE RINK

[MUSIC CUE 15A: WALLFLOWER PART II]

(*They dance.*)

ANNA. (*continued*) Dance, Angel. What about all those dance lessons I paid for?
ANGEL. Gee, ma, you'd think this was your prom.
ANNA. I never had one. (*They continue dancing.*) Watch this.
ANGEL. I can do that.
ANNA. I should hope so. It cost me four thousand dollars. Dance, Angel!
ANNA & ANGEL.
YOU'VE GOT TO STAND, BABY
TALL AND PROUD
GET NOTICED BY THE CROWD

SHAKE, BABY
MAKE 'EM BUZZ
AND YOU CAN BE A WHIZ THE WAY YOUR MAMA
  WAS

AND NOT A WALLFLOWER
WILTING IN THE NIGHT
HANDS ACROSS YOUR LAP
NOT HAVING ANY FUN AT ALL
  ANNA.
UP AGAINST THE WALL
  ANGEL.
GLUED AGAINST THE WALL
  ANNA & ANGEL.
PLASTERED TO THE WALL!

(*As the song ends, the snackbar turns around to reveal a banquette, where ANGEL and ANNA sit.*

Suddenly streamers, balloons and Hawaiian decorations come flying in. Up tempo, Rock and Roll dance music.)

[MUSIC CUE 15B: THE PROM]

(*Present at the dance are UNCLE FAUSTO, much older, SISTER PHILOMENA [BEN], BOBBY PERILLO [LUCKY], PETER REILLY [TONY], DEBBIE DUBERMAN [GUY], and JUNIOR MILLER [BUDDY]. We will have to imagine the rest of the party and see it through their eyes.*

DEBBIE and PETER are dancing near the organ. BOBBY crosses DS.C. to JUNIOR.)

BOBBY. I just wanna lay Debbie Duberman. Look at those mammeries!
SISTER PHILOMENA. Looking is all I better catch you doing, Bobby Perillo.
BOBBY. Good evening, Sister.

(*PETER and JUNIOR are sharing a joint.*)

ANNA. (*to SISTER PHILOMENA*) That's a lot of ankle we're showing tonight, Sister.
SISTER PHILOMENA. It's this new Pope. Today, the ankle; tomorrow the whole leg. Next thing you know, it'll be hot pants. I hope that's a cigarette I see you smoking, Junior Miller!
JUNIOR. It is, Sister! (*He swallows the joint. SISTER PHILOMENA hurries out the US.L. gate.*)
ANNA. Psst! There he is! (*She motions towards BOBBY PERILLO with a toss of her head. BOBBY is talking to DEBBIE near the organ.*)
ANGEL. Here goes nothing. (*She gets up and crosses the dance floor, passing through a group of high school boys.*)
PETER. Hey, Angel, you look great.
JUNIOR. Hot stuff.
ANGEL. The line forms over there. Excuse me. (*She goes up to BOBBY PERILLO and DEBBY DUBERMAN.*) Look at you, standing here like a wallflower, Bobby Perillo. Why don't you ask him to dance, Debby? Too shy? Watch how I do it. "Dance, Angel?" "I'd love to." Bye, Debby.

(*ANGEL and BOBBY start to dance. JUNIOR starts dancing with DEBBY. ANNA comes up to PETER.*)

ANNA. Come on, let's see what you can do.

(*ANNA dances with PETER. As the couples dance, ANNA and ANGEL give each other the high sign. ANGEL has done very well for herself. She's pleased. So is ANNA. Music up. The couples dance.*)

SISTER PHILOMENA. Bobby Perillo, where are you taking Angel Antonelli?

(*BOBBY has fox-trotted ANGEL into a dark, private corner US.R. and is trying to kiss and feel her up. UNCLE FAUSTO will follow them.*

UNCLE FAUSTO is seen scowling around the edges of the rink. He joins SISTER PHILOMENA.)

UNCLE FAUSTO. (*drunk, ugly mood*) I don't know which is worse: the rock and roll or the slow ones.
SISTER PHILOMENA. It's all in the eye of the beholder, Mr. Antonelli. (*She crosses out the US.L. gate.*)
UNCLE FAUSTO. (*derisively*) Is that what you call it?

(*Focus on DANCERS until ANGEL and BOBBY reappear DS.R. DEBBIE, PETER, and JUNIOR will move off during the following:*)

ANGEL. Don't, Bobby!
BOBBY. C'm'on, what's the matter?
ANGEL. I don't want to. (*They sit on the banquette.*)
BOBBY. Everybody else does.
ANGEL. I'm not everybody else. And neither are you.
BOBBY. Your mother said you liked me.
ANNA. (*observing the scene from US.C.*) I never said—.
ANGEL. I do like you. And she shouldn't have told you that.
BOBBY. Why not?
ANGEL. It's none of her—. You don't like me!
BOBBY. I do, Angel. I like you a lot.
ANGEL. You do?
BOBBY. Sure thing. That's why it's okay to . . . (*His hands are all over her again.*)
ANGEL. You like me? You're not just saying it to . . .
BOBBY. I'm crazy about you.
ANGEL. I want to believe you.
BOBBY. What do I have to do? (*He starts to kiss her.*)
UNCLE FAUSTO. (*from somewhere in the shadows*) You want a real man to show you, little boy?
ANGEL. Stop, Bobby! Somebody's there!

(*We hear UNCLE FAUSTO's hideous, drunken laughter from somewhere in the shadows.*)

UNCLE FAUSTO. (*appearing* DS.R.) These kids today. They don't even know how to make love.
ANGEL. It's my uncle. He's drunk. Come on, let's go.

(*She begins to lead BOBBY* L.)

UNCLE FAUSTO switches on a harsh overhead light. His shirt is out of his trousers. It should look like he's been playing with himself.)

UNCLE FAUSTO. What's your rush, little girl? Hunh? Where you go?
BOBBY. Hello, Mr. Antonelli. Angel and I were just . . .
UNCLE FAUSTO. I know what you were just. Only she said no. She's good. She's too good. You shoulda danced her mother in here. That one delivers, like a pro.
ANNA. Pig.
ANGEL. (*crossing* R. *towards FAUSTO*) If my father were alive, he'd kill you.
UNCLE FAUSTO. You're the only one in the whole amusement park who believes that dumb story your mother's been handing out.
BOBBY. (*trying to pull ANGEL* L. *away from FAUSTO*) Don't listen to him, Angel.
UNCLE FAUSTO. (*crossing* L. *to ANGEL*) Your father's alive.
ANGEL. What?
UNCLE FAUSTO. You tell her! They all know.
ANGEL. Shut up, just shut up.
UNCLE FAUSTO. They all know and they're all laughing at you.
ANGEL. I hate you. (*She pushes him down on the banquette.*) Where is he?
UNCLE FAUSTO. I don't know.
ANGEL. Where is he?
UNCLE FAUSTO. I don't know. (*She slaps him. He pushes her to the floor. BOBBY has run off* US.L.) Okay. I'll tell you. Your father was a bum with a hard-on for every piece of tail on the boardwalk. And your mother is just this far from being an out and out tramp.
ANGEL. So what does that make me?
UNCLE FAUSTO. Somebody's dumb, fat, ugly mistake. You should be grateful to me. It's about time somebody told you the truth.

[MUSIC CUE 16: ALL THE CHILDREN IN A ROW]

(*He goes. ANGEL takes out a suitcase and frantically begins to pack it.*)

ANNA. How many times do I have to tell you? Your father died when you were six years old.

ANGEL. You're a liar. A liar.

ANNA. Angel, please. (*They have a "tug-o-war" with the clothes.*)

ANGEL. I hate you. I hate you with every ounce and inch of me. He must have, too! It's your fault he left. It's like you murdered him. (*She closes the suitcase.*)

ANNA. I wish I had.

ANGEL. I'll never forgive you.

ANNA. You don't mean that, Angel.

ANGEL. (*hysterically*) He was my father!

ANNA. (*powerfully*) He was my life. I worshipped him. I gave him all the love I had in me. There wasn't any left for anybody else.

ANGEL. Including me.

ANNA. Including me! Where are you going?

ANGEL. Somewhere, someplace someone like you will never find me.

(*Light change. The prom decorations fly away, and ANGEL seems to be alone, suitcase in hand, somewhere other than the rink.*)

ANGEL.
ALL THE CHILDREN IN A ROW
LEAVING HOME BEHIND
WE'VE A WAR TO WIN, YOU KNOW
WE'VE A LIFE TO FIND
HAVE YOU BEEN TO MONTEREY
DIDN'T JANIS SING?
KESEY'S BUS CAME BY TODAY
STEPPENWOLF IS KING

ALL THE CHILDREN IN A ROW
FLOWERS IN THEIR HAIR
WHY DO PEOPLE TURN AWAY?
MAN, IT ISN'T FAIR

LEARY'S IN THE SLAMMER NOW
BOY, IS THAT A MESS
LIGHT A MATCH AND BURN THE CARD
DOCTOR SPOCK SAYS "YES"

MARCHING PROUDLY ARM IN ARM
SINGING DYLAN SONGS
NO ONE IS A STRANGER HERE
EVERYONE BELONGS

CALIFORNIA'S WARM AS LOVE
I'M WITH FRIENDS, I KNOW
IN THE GALLANT ARMY OF
ALL THE CHILDREN IN A ROW

WHO CAN CHANGE THINGS? WE CAN!
WHO WILL CHANGE THINGS? WE WILL!

(*A young hippie DANNY [LUCKY] appears* US.C. *and slowly crosses* DS. *to ANGEL.*)

AND ME AND DANNY RUNNING HAND-IN-HAND
FRISBEES ON THE SAND
   DANNY. Wanna be my old lady? Whaddaya say?
   ANGEL.
ME AND DANNY
BURGERS ON A BUN
BANNERS IN THE SUN
   DANNY. Might as well be my old lady. Everybody says you are anyway!
   ANGEL.
TURNING IN THE NIGHT, HUNGRY
   DANNY.
LOOKIT, YOU'RE MY WIFE, AIN'T YOU?
PROMISE NOT TO LAUGH, WILL YOU?
ANSWER ME ONE THING, HONEST
PLEASE DON'T TELL A SOUL I ASKED YOU
WHERE'S CAMBODIA?
   ANGEL.
ME AND DANNY, WALKING DOWN THE STREET
"HOW WE GONNA EAT?"
   DANNY. Dudes who ain't got no old lady—they move on, you know.

ANGEL.
ME AND DANNY, WHY'D YOU PICK THAT FIGHT?
NO, IT'S NOT ALL RIGHT
WE WERE BRAVE TOGETHER, STRONG TOGETHER
WHERE'S IT GONE?

(*DANNY is backing away.*)

DO YOU NEED TO TAKE THAT STUFF?
COME ON, DANNY, THAT'S ENOUGH
WE CAN MAKE IT, WE'LL SURVIVE
DANNY, YOU'RE TOO STONED TO DRIVE!

(*The music sounds like a car crash. In the distance a siren wails. DANNY is gone.*)

ANNA. I'm sorry, honey, I didn't know.
ANGEL.
ME AND DANNY, I DON'T UNDERSTAND
WHERE'S THE WORLD WE PLANNED?
ANNA. I'm sorry, honey.
ANGEL.
IN CALIFORNIA, IT DOESN'T EVER SNOW
IN CALIFORNIA, LIVING'S KIND OF SLOW

(*Lights and music change. A much older DINO appears* US.L., *and crosses* DS.)

DINO. (*Pause; ANGEL stares.*) Yeah? You want to see me? What's the matter with you?

(*ANNA, on the stairs, apart from ANGEL and DINO in her own light and space, is "seeing DINO," too.*)

ANNA. Dino? Is that you? (*Truly, she doesn't know whether to laugh or cry.*)
ANGEL. It's me, papa.
DINO. Angel? You were supposed to think I was dead.
ANGEL. Oh, Papa, I never really believed that. Never. I've been looking all over for you. I hate her, Papa. I have different reasons, but I think I hate her more than you do.
DINO. Don't hate your mother. I never did. (*He crosses* R. *ANGEL follows.*) How old are you now?

ANGEL. Twenty-three.

DINO. You're a nice looking girl.

ANGEL. Thank you.

DINO. (*at* DS.R.) I guess the boys go for you?

ANGEL. Oh, papa, why did you leave us?

DINO. I don't know.

ANGEL. I need an answer.

DINO. I didn't belong there. But look at you! You turned out fine.

ANGEL. How would you know?

DINO. Hey, I'm being nice.

ANGEL. I haven't turned out nice, papa. Couldn't you just hold me?

DINO. What'd be the point?

ANNA. (*remembering*) What'd be the point?

DINO. Listen, Angel, I can't . . .

ANGEL. I don't want anything. Just hold—.

DINO. It's too late for you. I'm sorry. (*crossing below ANGEL to* C. *stage*) I've got a family . . . two boys.

ANNA. (*to herself*) They all want sons.

DINO. What are you? One of them hippies, I guess? . . . Quit staring at me like that, will you? I'm only human!

ANGEL. Papa, I'm pregnant.

ANNA. (*on the steps*) Sweet Jesus!

DINO. I didn't hear that. You didn't say it and I didn't hear it. Capisce? Look, do me a favor and don't come back. It ain't fair to either one of us.

(*He goes off* US.L.

Music up. Lights change. ANGEL picks up her suitcase and crosses DS.C., *where she is isolated in a light.*)

ANGEL.
ALL THE CHILDREN IN A ROW
CONFIDENT AND BRAVE
WE'VE A WAR TO WIN, YOU KNOW
WE'VE A WORLD TO SAVE

NO ONE THINKS WE MATTER MUCH
NO ONE UNDERSTANDS
BUT WE MADE A DIFFERENCE BY
THE JOINING OF OUR HANDS

CALIFORNIA'S WARM AS LOVE
I BELONG, I KNOW
TO THE GALLANT ARMY OF
ALL THE CHILDREN IN A ROW!

(*backing* US.)

WHO KEEPS MARCHING? WE DO!
WHO'S THE FUTURE? WE ARE!
WE ARE!
WE
ARE!

(*She puts the suitcase down and sits on it.*

Lights change abruptly, returning us to "the present." ANNA steps forward.)

ANNA. (*crossing down* R. *to ANGEL's left*) You were pregnant the last time you were home?
ANGEL. (*rising and moving away from her mother*) It must have slipped my mind.
ANNA. Why didn't you tell me?
ANGEL. For the same reason you never told me a lot of things. I came home to, but we don't talk. We yell, we scream, we hurt, we hate. We do everything but talk.
ANNA. It was this Danny's?
ANGEL. (*nodding*) Daniel Heathcliff Waverly Scott. A Scorpio from Harrisburg, Pa., with a minor in Italian.
ANNA. I guess you did what most young women do nowadays?
ANGEL. What do you think?
ANNA. I can't say that I blame you.
ANGEL. Thanks. (*She turns away from her.*)
ANNA. Angel!
ANGEL. (*crossing near the organ*) You'll miss your plane.

[MUSIC CUE 16A: GARAGE DOOR]

(*The outside door to the rink has opened. The same blinding morning light as before.*)

ANNA. I'm closed. (*She squints and sees that a LITTLE GIRL is standing there.*) I said we're closed, honey.

LITTLE GIRL. I'm looking for my mother.
ANGEL. (*crossing* US.C. *to the child*) What are you doing here?
LITTLE GIRL. I got tired waiting.
ANGEL. How did you get here?
LITTLE GIRL. I took a cab.
ANGEL. Where did you get the money to take a cab?
LITTLE GIRL. I didn't. I need five dollars. (*The LITTLE GIRL turns to ANNA.*) Hello. Who are you?
ANNA. I think I'm your grandmother.
LITTLE GIRL. You think? (*to ANGEL*) You're right. She's far out for an old lady.
ANGEL. Honey, cool it. (*giving LITTLE GIRL money*) Take this out to him and ask him to wait.
LITTLE GIRL. We're not staying?
ANGEL. We'll see.
LITTLE GIRL. This is six dollars.
ANGEL. It's for a tip.
LITTLE GIRL. Are you kidding? He called this place a dump. It is, but I didn't appreciate him saying it.
ANGEL. You're right. Give me my buck back.
LITTLE GIRL. (*to ANNA*) I'd kiss you but I don't know you well enough yet and she's raising me not to be a hypocrite.
ANNA. In the meantime, what do I call you?
LITTLE GIRL. Anna.
ANNA. (*looking at ANGEL*) Yeah? I'm Anna, too.
LITTLE GIRL. What's the matter?
ANNA. Did anybody ever tell you you were gorgeous?
LITTLE GIRL. My mama. All the time. (*She goes.*)
ANNA. She's beautiful.
ANGEL. I know.
ANNA. You were gonna leave without me knowing I had a granddaughter?
ANGEL. *You* were gonna leave. I wanted her to grow up here. I wanted her to have all this.
ANNA. Anna! You named her Anna.
ANGEL. It's a nice name. (*She turns away from ANNA.*)
ANNA. Why can't you forgive me?
ANGEL. It's not that easy. We're talking about my whole life.
ANNA. We're talking about the past. Let go of it. What are you afraid of?
ANGEL. There won't be anything there.
ANNA. There will be. You gotta trust. We both do. "It's okay, ma". That's all you gotta say. "It's okay".

ANGEL. It's not okay!

ANNA. Angel, I'm sorry I lied about your father. I'm sorry about the other men. I'm sorry I never told you you were pretty. I'm sorry you didn't know how much I love you. I love you, Angel. Tell me you love me.

ANGEL. You know I do.

ANNA. Some things you gota *hear.*

ANGEL. All right, I love you. (*turning away*) Now go to hell.

ANNA. Not until you tell me: "It's okay." Look at me.

ANGEL. It's okay!

ANNA. It's okay, ma. (*After a very long pause, ANGEL looks at her mother.*)

ANGEL. (*finally*) It's okay, ma. It's okay. It's okay. It's okay. It's okay.

(*She is sobbing uncontrollably. So is ANNA. It is impossible to say who moves first but they are in each other's arms.*)

[MUSIC CUE 17: FINALE ACT II]

ANNA. Thank you. It's okay, Angel. It's okay.

(*THE WRECKERS have appeared and are watching silently. The phone begins to ring.*)

ANGEL. You're right. It's the past I was holding onto. It's not about the rink.

ANNA. Right now it is. (*They both look at the phone.*)

LINO. So what's the verdict?

ANGEL. (*to ANNA, confidentially*) How much did you say we got for this place?

ANNA. A lot of money.

ANGEL. A lot of money?

ANNA. I'll put it this way: the kid won't be selling apples. (*A car horn sounds outside.*)

ANGEL. Ma, where's Lenny in all this?

ANNA. Lenny always wanted a family. Well now he's got one.

ANGEL. Ah ma!

ANNA. Don't worry about us. We're fine. It's everybody else who's screwed up.

(*ANGEL goes to the still-ringing phone, picks up the receiver, and tosses it away.*)

ANGEL. (*to THE WRECKERS*) She's all yours! (*THE WRECKERS exit onto the boardwalk.*)

ANNA.
HERE'S TO THE RINK
AND ALL OF US TOGETHER

ANGEL.
AND ALL OF US TOGETHER

ANNA.
I'LL DRINK TO THAT!

ANGEL.
I'LL DRINK TO THAT!

ANNA & ANGEL.
I'LL DRINK TO THAT
I'LL DRINK TO THAT!

(*We hear the organ vamp again. The women embrace. ANNA leads ANGEL to the stairs. Lights change, and the entire rink breaks free from its foundation and gracefully lifts up, away, and out of sight, leaving nothing but the boardwalk, the sea and the sky. ANGEL calls to her daughter.*)

ANGEL. Anna!

(*The LITTLE GIRL comes running on and joins them on the stairs, ANNA at the top, ANGEL below her, and the LITTLE GIRL below ANGEL. The three generations join hands and turn to face the world outside, silhouetted against the sky. Curtain.*)

[MUSIC CUE 18: BOWS]

[MUSIC CUE 19: EXIT MUSIC]

COMPLETE MUSIC CUE RUNNING ORDER

1. Colored Lights
1A. Colored Lights Underscore (Playoff)
1B. Wreckers' Entrance
2. Chief Cook and Bottle Washer
2A. Angel's Entrance
3. Don't Ah Ma Me
4. Blue Crystal
4A. Blue Crystal/Korea
5. Familiar Things
5A. Blue Crystal Underscore
6. Not Enough Magic
7. We Can Make It
8. After All These Years
9. Angel's Rink (and Social Center)
10. What Happened to the Old Days?
10A. Finale Act I (Colored Lights Reprise)

10B. Entr'Acte
11. The Apple Doesn't Fall
12. Marry Me
12A. Arnie's Underscore
12B. Blue Crystal/Korea
13. We Can Make It (Reprise)
13A. Quintet Part I/Part II
14. The Rink
15. Wallflower Part I
15A. Wallflower Part II
15B. The Prom
16. All the Children in a Row
16A. Garage Door
17. Finale Act II (Coda)
18. Bows
19. Exit Music

COSTUME PLOT
(Broadway Production)

GUY (Scott Holmes)

1. SKATER — blue short-sleaved shirt, blue striped pants — *skates*
2. WRECKER — tan coveralls, burgundy knit cap — *top sider shoes*
3. DINO ("Blue Crystal") — blue silk shirt (solid), skater pants — *black slip-ons*
4. DINO #2 (Korea) — tan & brown 50's shirt, same pants — *same shoes*
5. DINO #3 (Mirror ball) — Army uniform, hat, tie, belt — *black tie up*
6. REPEAT WRECKER ("All these Years"/ "Angel's Rink") — (repeat #2 above)

Intermission

7. DINO #4 (before wedding) — gray pleated pants, white t-shirt, maroon jacket — *repeat black tie up*
8. DINO #5 (wedding) — one-piece jumpsuit, wedding jacket — *same shoes*
9. DINO #6 (fight) — 50's blue & white plaid shirt (solid sleaves), same pants — *same shoes*
10. PRIEST ("Quintet") — black priest's robe & neck piece — *same shoes*
11. REPEAT WRECKER ("The Rink") — (repeat #2 above)
12. DEBBIE DUBERMAN (prom) — yellow prom dress, long gloves, necklace, earrings — *carry yellow high heels*

13. OLD DINO ("All the Children in a Row")	padded t-shirt, pajama bottoms, brown & yellow plaid robe	*slippers*
14. REPEAT WRECKER (Finale)	(repeat #2 above)	

LINO (Jason Alexander)

1. WRECKER	tan windbreaker, tan cap, beige corduroy pants, gray hooded sweat shirt, beige leather gloves, brown leather work belt	*work boots*
2. LENNY (Mirror ball)	light green shirt, rust print bow tie, light rust plaid jacket, green sharkskin pants	*brown tie-up*
3. REPEAT WRECKER ("All These Years"/ "Angel's Rink")	(repeat #1 above)	
4. PUNK (boardwalk)	rust pants, blue leather vest, black sweat shirt, green beret, sun glasses, leather wrist bands	*green sneakers*

Intermission

5. LENNY #2 ("Marry Me")	blue plaid jacket, solid blue gaberdine pants, shirt/vest/tie (all-in-one)	*brown tie-up*
6. UNCLE FAUSTO	brown/green suit w/yellow & red plaid shirt and tie (all-in-one)	*same shoes*
7. FAUSTO #2 (wedding)	one-piece wedding jumpsuit w/jacket	*black shoes*

8. LENNY #3 ("Quintet")	green & brown houndstooth jacket, brown pants, brown print bow tie, pink striped shirt	*loafers*
9. REPEAT WRECKER ("The Rink")	(repeat #1 above)	
10. FAUSTO #3 (prom)	brown pants w/stripe, yellow & black flannel shirt, suspenders	*brown shoes*
11. REPEAT WRECKER (Finale)	(repeat #1 above)	

BEN (Ronn Carroll)

1. WRECKER	blue striped overalls, blue & red flannel shirt, blue jeans jacket, rust suede work gloves	*work boots*
2. DINO'S FATHER (Korea)	brown plaid pants, gray & red striped shirt, brown vest w/watch fob	*brown tie-up*
3. FATHER #2 (Mirror ball)	same pants, pink & green striped shirt, brown/gray sweater vest	*same shoes*
4. REPEAT WRECKER	(repeat #1 above)	
5. MRS. SILVERMAN (boardwalk)	blue & gold print dress, hat, beige purse, bracelets, earrings	*brown pumps*

Intermission

6. FATHER #3	brown gaberdine coat, brown plaid pants, maroon scarf, brown fedora	*brown shoes*
7. FATHER #4 (wedding)	all-in-one jumpsuit, jacket	*black shoes*

8. FATHER #5 ("If you do this")	pants w/suspenders, white t-shirt, open brown plaid flannel/wool shirt	*brown shoes*
9. REPEAT WRECKER ("The Rink")	(repeat #1 above)	
10. SISTER PHILOMENA (prom)	gray nun's dress, black hat, gold cross	*black nun's shoes*
11. REPEAT WRECKER (Finale)	(repeat #1 above)	

BUDDY (Mel Johnson, Jr.)

1. WRECKER	green army fatigues, maroon striped cotton shirt, rosy sweater vest, leather work belt, gray cotton baseball jacket	*work boots*
2. HIRAM (Mirror ball)	Army uniform, hat, belt, tie	*black shoes*
3. REPEAT WRECKER ("All These Years"/ "Angel's Rink")	(repeat #1 above)	
4. MRS. JACKSON (boardwalk)	maroon print dress, beige cardigan sweater, hat, purse, bracelets, earrings	*brown pumps*

Intermission

5. REPEAT WRECKER ("Apple")	(repeat #1 above)	

6.	CHARLIE	navy wool baseball jacket, brown pants, striped cotton polo shirt	*loafers*
7.	WEDDING	3-piece black tuxedo, white formal shirt, cummerbund, tie	*black shoes*
8.	QUINTET	brown pants, brown striped sports coat, green sweater vest attached to shirt	*loafers*
9.	REPEAT WRECKER ("The Rink")	(repeat #1 above)	
10.	JUNIOR MILLER (prom)	white dinner jacket, black tux pants, white formal shirt, blue vest	*black shoes*
11.	REPEAT WRECKER (Finale)	(repeat #1 above)	

LUCKY (Scott Ellis)

1.	WRECKER	blue denim jean vest, rust work gloves, beige long sleeve thermal shirt, gray washed-out jeans, brown work belt	*work boots*
2.	SUGAR (Mirror ball)	off-red 50's party dress, hat, gloves, bracelets, fur stole, beaded purse	*red & beige pumps*
3.	REPEAT WRECKER ("All These Years"/ "Angel's Rink")	(repeat #1 above)	
4.	PUNK (boardwalk)	sweatpants, belt, black shiny top, net top over shoulder blades, headband	*red sneakers*

Intermission

5. ARNIE	green pants, mauve striped t-shirt, tan 40's jacket	black shoes
6. WEDDING	3-piece tuxedo, white formal shirt, black bow tie, cummerbund	
7. QUINTET	faded blue pants, blue plaid shirt, tan leather jacket	loafers
8. REPEAT WRECKER ("The Rink")	(repeat #1 above)	
9. BOBBY PERILLO (prom)	white formal jacket, yellow formal shirt, black tux pants, bow tie	black shoes
10. DANNY ("All the Children in a Row")	green Army fatigues, tie-dyed open t-shirt, headband, turquoise necklace	no shoes
11. REPEAT WRECKER (Finale)	(repeat #1 above)	

TONY (Frank Mastrocola)

1. WRECKER	gray sleeveless sweatshirt w/red neckband, gray sweatshirt vest, tan cotton baseball jacket, blue jeans, green work gloves, brown leather belt	work boots
2. TOM (Mirror ball)	peach shirt, green & rust tie, brown pants, turquoise & yellow striped jacket	brown & cream capezio shoes
3. REPEAT WRECKER ("All These Years"/ "Angel's Rink")	(repeat #1 above)	
4. PUNK (boardwalk)	lavender t-shirt, green jeans, red knit top, maroon knit cap	black sneakers

Intermission

5. **REPEAT WRECKER** (repeat #1 above)
   ("Apple")
6. **WEDDING** 3-piece black tuxedo, white formal shirt, black bow tie & cummerbund — *black shoes*
7. **QUINTET** tan striped pants, gray & mauve knit shirt
8. **REPEAT WRECKER** (repeat #1 above)
   ("The Rink")
9. **PETER REILLY** white dinner jacket, black tux pants, white formal shirt, bow tie — *black shoes*
   (prom)
10. **REPEAT WRECKER** (repeat #1 above)
    (Finale)

ANNA (Chita Rivera)

silk shirtwaist dress — lavender w/beige irregular dots — long sleeves, wraparound waist closing (no zipper) — *women's character high heel (2½") dance shoes — two-tone spectators: beige w/lavender toe & heel*

ANGEL (Liza Minelli)

blue jeans (straight leg) w/patches; black & red tie-dyed scoop-necked t-shirt, long sleeves; blue denim shirt w/embroidery; burnt-orange Eddie Bauer all-weather hiking jacket; 3 long antique scarves around neck; red bandanna rolled as headband

Fried's of London jazz shoes—purple

LITTLE GIRL (Kim Hauser)

1. COLORED LIGHTS

powder blue skating dress w/puffed sleeves, Peter Pan collar, and full-length skirt (mid-thigh); ruffled panties; white tights

white skates

2. FINALE

blue jeans; red, white, and blue striped t-shirt; hooded zippered sweatshirt; blue jean jacket

sneakers

PROPERTY PLOT

STAGE LEFT

4 Coke cases w/newspapers on top (Boston area)
Long Coca-Cola sign
Coke cooler (long, low 50's type w/door on top)
Tool box on casters: (large enough to hold a person inside); 10' roll bubble paper (inside); wooden mallet (inside)
Medium size crowbar
Wulitzer juke box
Wooden crate w/dime taped on top
Plastic shopping bag
Ghetto blaster
Money (small bills)
Wooden skate case
Antique skates w/wooden wheels
Case of full coke bottles
Dishtowel
Loaf Italian bread in paper wrapper
Lucky's skates
Guy's skates
Wooden crate: Buddy's skates; Tony's skates
2 sets Hawaiian leis
3 lunchboxes
Gum
Cigarettes
Joints
Zippo lighters

(Act I preset)

Plastic drop cloth hung over organ
Dime on organ
Ben's R. skate US. organ
Ben's L. skate in L.1
Stool (L.1)
Crash box (L.1)
Trunk covered w/plastic drop cloth (inside L. back wall)

(Act I preset, escape platform)

6-pack beer (1 w/water inside)
Blue crystal glass
2 50's table lamps

Contract
Box of toys w/old teddy bear on top
Hula hoop
50's floor lamp

(Act II preset)

Skate ramp & trick skate (L.1)
2 kitchen chairs (escape plat)
Large suitcase (escape)
Large shoulder bag (escape)

STAGE RIGHT

Rolling Stone newspaper — 1977
Suitcase ⎫
Duffle bag ⎬ pre-set in front of house curtain prior to hour
Knapsack ⎭
2 Granola bars (pre-set in knapsack)
Tray w/7 blue crystal glasses & 1 breakable blue crystal look-a-like
Magic mirror ball
Magic mirror ball gift wrapped box
Teddy bear
Yellow shopping bag w/4 high beam flash lites set in shopping bag
1 Ghetto blaster
2 Trick skates
Cushioned kneeler pillow
Misle
2 Sets of Hawaiian leis
Child's knapsack
Child's walkman
Clip board w/pencil, paper, and large key ring w/keys
Wreckers knapsack
Paper back book
Wreckers flashlites
Paper bag w/2 cardboard cups of coffee
Cigarettes
Zippo lighters
Cocaine bottle, razor blade

THE RINK

(Pre-sets)

Cigarettes & lighter at pay phone
Cigarettes & lighter at up center platform
Powder puff in compact at bottom of stairs
Dime on up center platform
Dime on organ

(Snack Bar Pre-set)

Ash tray
Coke-a-cola bottle w/straw
Brioschi bottle
Cola glass w/water
Champagne bottle, corked and foiled
2 dish towels
10 pieces of boston area newspaper (for wrapping glasses)
Tall glass of water
Cardboard box w/8 slots; 5 slots w/newspaper wrapped blue crystal glasses; 3 slots, empty
Crash drawer to break blue crystal glass
Soda fountain spigets
Large plastic drop cloth to cover snack bar

(Back Bar Pre-set)

Orange Crush machine
Orange squeezer
Malted milk mixer
10 Stacks of large colorful soda cups
Hot dog roasting machine

(Act II Pre-set)

5 Joints and lighter in duffle bag
Duffle bag set behind house curtain, center stage
Strike tool box
Set skate chute in right wing

"CHIEF COOK AND BOTTLE WASHER" Preset:

(Stage Right)

4-Wheeled luggage cart w/crate, hemp, grappling hoods, & roll of bubble paper

THE RINK

2 15' rolls of bubble paper
5 Flat boxes marked "fragile"
Red tool box
2 Wooden dollys
Tool box
Industrial electrical extension cord
10' Aluminum ladder
2 Hand trucks
Coiled hemp
Crowbar — green (med size)
2 Flat boxes

(Stage Left)

Sled
Roll of linoleum
7-UP sign
3 signs: Hires; Mason's Root Beer; Kist
Hand truck: 3 coke cases; 2 gumball machines
Marquee letters: A, E, L
Rolled-up carpet
2 Signs: round Coca-Cola & Mission Orange

(Escape Platform [upstairs])

Box w/lamp inside
Trick lampshade (can be worn on head)
Birdcage

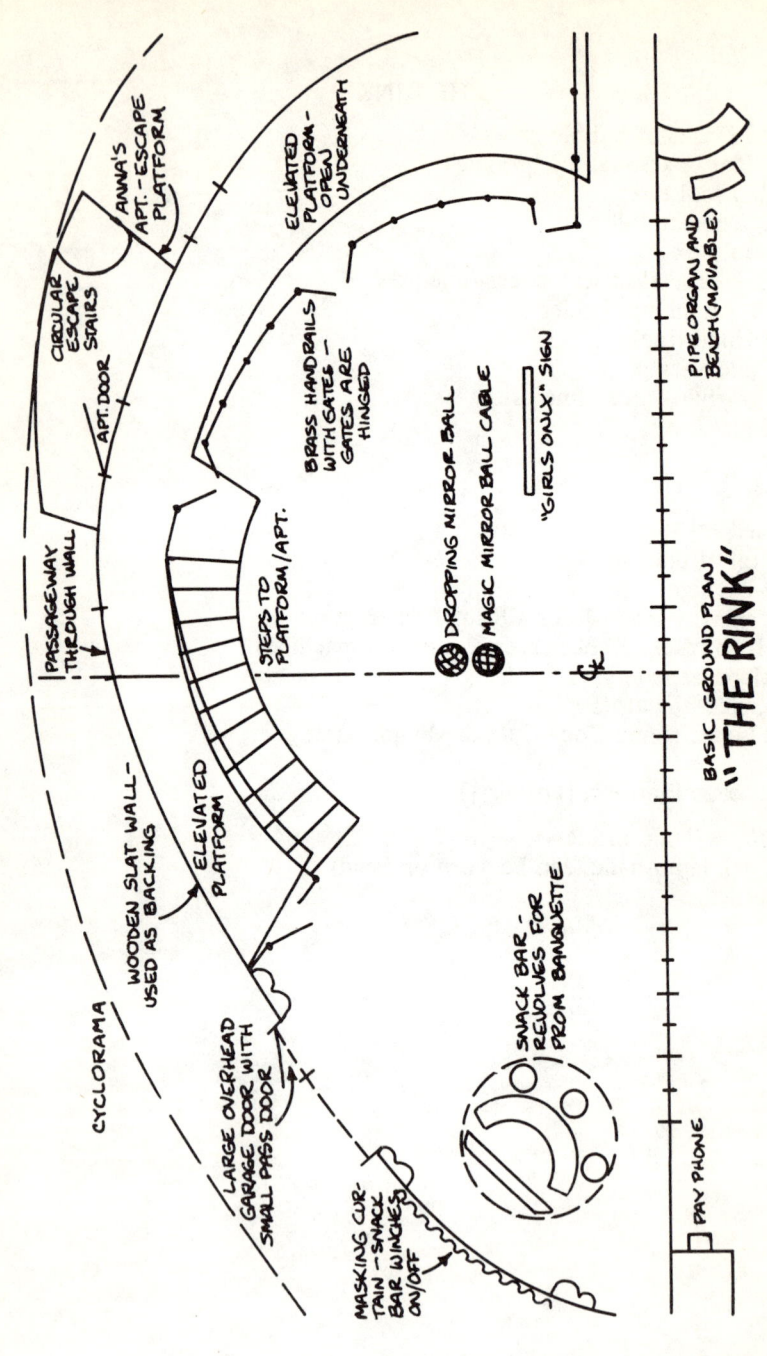

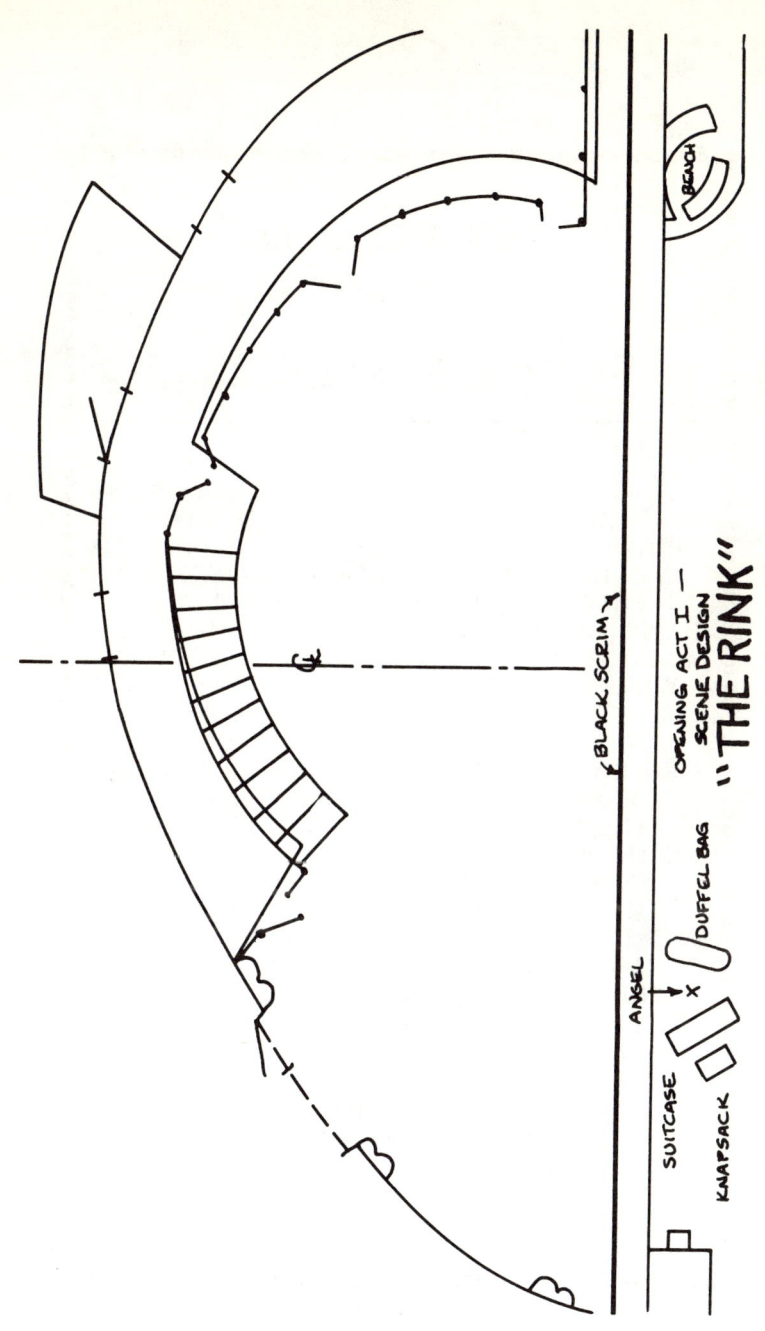

NEW MUSICALS
from
SAMUEL FRENCH, INC.

BALLROOM – THE BEST LITTLE WHOREHOUSE IN TEXAS – CHICAGO – CHRISTMAS IS COMIN' UPTOWN – THE CLUB – COLE – THE DRACULA SPECTACULAR – DRACULA: THE *MUSICAL*? – FESTIVAL – THE FIRST – GOLD DUST – HAPPY END – HAPPY NEW YEAR – HIJINKS! – A HISTORY OF THE AMERICAN FILM – I LOVE MY WIFE – I'M GETTING MY ACT TOGETHER AND TAKING IT ON THE ROAD – JERRY'S GIRLS – KURT VONNEGUT'S GOD BLESS YOU MR. ROSEWATER – MARCH OF THE FALSETTOS – MUSICAL CHAIRS – MY OLD FRIENDS – THE 1940'S RADIO HOUR – OH, BROTHER! ON THE TWENTIETH CENTURY – OPERETTA – PETTICOAT LANE – PIAF – PIANO BAR – THE PICTURE OF DORIAN GRAY – PUMP BOYS AND DINETTES – THE ROCKY HORROR SHOW – RUNAWAYS – THE SALOONKEEPER'S DAUGHTER – THE SEVEN – STRIDER – SUGAR BABIES – THEY'RE PLAYING OUR SONG – TRIXIE TRUE, TEEN DETECTIVE – UNSUNG COLE (AND CLASSICS, TOO) – THE UTTER GLORY OF MORRISSEY HALL – THE WIZ – WOMAN OVERBOARD – YOU NEVER KNOW

For descriptions of these and all our musicals consult our Musicals Catalogue, available FREE.

NEW MUSICALS
from
SAMUEL FRENCH, INC.

ALICE IN CONCERT—A . . . MY NAME IS ALICE—AND ON THE SIXTH DAY—ANDY CAPP—ANIMAL CRACKERS—THE BIOGRAPH GIRL—CHARLOTTE SWEET—A DAY IN HOLLYWOOD/A NIGHT IN THE UKRAINE—A DOLL'S LIFE—DRACULA: THE *MUSICAL*?—THE DRACULA SPECTACULA—THE HAGGADAH—HEAD OVER HEELS—THE HEEBIE JEEBIES—THE HUMAN COMEDY—IS THERE LIFE AFTER HIGH SCHOOL?—JEKYLL HYDES AGAIN—THE JUNIPER TREE—LITTLE SHOP OF HORRORS—MARCH OF THE FALSETTOS—MISS LIBERTY—NINE—NOT *THE* COUNT OF MONTE CRISTO?—PREPPIES—REALLY ROSIE—THE RINK—SERIOUS BIZNESS—SONGBOOK—TAKING MY TURN—TOMFOOLERY—WOMAN OF THE YEAR

For descriptions of these and all our fine musicals, consult our MUSICALS CATALOGUE, available FREE!

FAVORITE MUSICALS from
"THE HOUSE OF PLAYS"

BALLROOM – THE BEST LITTLE WHOREHOUSE IN TEXAS – CHICAGO – CHRISTMAS IS COMIN' UPTOWN – THE CLUB – DAMES AT SEA – DIAMOND STUDS – EL GRANDE DE COCA COLA – GREASE A HISTORY OF THE AMERICAN FILM – I LOVE MY WIFE – I'M GETTING MY ACT TOGETHER AND TAKING IT ON THE ROAD – LITTLE MARY SUNSHINE – THE ME NOBODY KNOWS – OF THEE I SING – ON THE TWENTIETH CENTURY – PETER PAN – PURLIE – RAISIN – RUNAWAYS – SEESAW – SHENANDOAH – SOMETHING'S AFOOT – STRIDER – THEY'RE PLAYING OUR SONG – THE WIZ

Consult our *Musicals Catalogue* for details.

ON THE TWENTIETH CENTURY
(ALL GROUPS—MUSICAL COMEDY)

Book and Lyrics by ADOLPH GREEN and BETTY COMDEN, Music by CY COLEMAN

17 principal roles, plus singers and extras (doubling possible)—Various sets

Whether performed with elaborate scenery, or on a simple skeletal scale, this brilliantly comic musical can appeal to audiences everywhere. This is truly an extravagant show—but its extravagance lies not in its scenery and physical production, but in the boisterous, tumultuous energy—and in the lush and sprightly energetic surge of its very melodic score. The story concerns the efforts of a flamboyant theatrical impressario to persuade a film star to appear in his next production, to outwit rival producers and creditors, to rid himself of religious nut Letitia Primrose (played by Imogene Coca on Broadway) and Lily's film star boyfriend Bruce Granit (who's as strong in profile as he is weak in brains). And, he must do all this before the famed 20th Century Ltd. reaches NYC! The story, and it's two leading characters—the mad impressario Oscar Jaffe and the love of his life and his greatest star Lily Garland—can be loved and enjoyed by all audiences. "Spectacular . . . funny . . . elegant . . . civilized wit and wild humor."—N.Y. Times. "A perfect musical . . . a gorgeous show!"—N.Y. Post. (#819)

KURT VONNEGUT'S GOD BLESS YOU, MR. ROSEWATER
(MUSICAL SATIRE)

By the creators of LITTLE SHOP OF HORRORS

Book and Lyrics by HOWARD ASHMAN
Music by ALAN MENKEN
Additional lyrics by DENNIS GREEN

10 men, 4 women (principals—also double smaller roles), extras, musicians—Various interiors and exteriors

"One of Vonnegut's most affecting and likeable novels becomes an affecting and likable theatrical experience, with more inventiveness, cockeyed characters, high-muzzle-velocity dialogue and just plain energy that you get from the majority of playwrights."—Newsweek. Eliot Rosewater's a well-intentioned idealist and philanthropic nut—and as president of a multi-million family foundation dispenses money to arcane and artsy-crafty projects. He's also a World War II veteran with a guilt complex, haunted by all this wealth—and also slightly crazy. His outlandish behavior enrages his senator dad, alienates his society-conscious wife—and the money attracts a young, shyster lawyer who tries to divert it to an obscure branch of the family. It portrays Vonnegut's vision of money, avarice and human behavior—as it aims a satirical fusillade at plastic America, fast foods, trademarks, slogans, media blitzes and the follies of materialism. "A charming, delightful, unexpected and thoughtful musical."—N.Y. Post. (#630)

FAVORITE BROADWAY COMEDIES *from* SAMUEL FRENCH, INC.

BAREFOOT IN THE PARK – BEDROOM FARCE – BLITHE SPIRIT – BUTTERFLIES ARE FREE – CALIFORNIA SUITE – CHAMPAGNE COMPLEX – CHAPTER TWO – COME BLOW YOUR HORN – DA – THE GINGERBREAD LADY – GOD'S FAVORITE – THE GOOD DOCTOR – HAPPY BIRTHDAY, WANDA JUNE – HAY FEVER – HOW THE OTHER HALF LOVES – I OUGHT TO BE IN PICTURES – JUMPERS – KNOCK KNOCK – LAST OF THE RED HOT LOVERS – MY FAT FRIEND – NEVER TOO LATE – NIGHT AND DAY – THE NORMAN CONQUESTS – NORMAN, IS THAT YOU? – THE ODD COUPLE – OTHERWISE ENGAGED – THE OWL AND THE PUSSYCAT – THE PRISONER OF 2ND AVENUE – THE PRIVATE EAR AND THE PUBLIC EYE – THE RAINMAKER – SAME TIME, NEXT YEAR – THE SHOW OFF – 6 RMS RIV VU – THE SUNSHINE BOYS – A THOUSAND CLOWNS – TRAVESTIES – TWIGS – TWO FOR THE SEASAW

For descriptions of these and all our plays, consult our Basic Catalogue of Plays.

Other Publications for Your Interest

A WEEKEND NEAR MADISON
(LITTLE THEATRE—COMIC DRAMA)
By KATHLEEN TOLAN

2 men, 3 women—Interior

This recent hit from the famed Actors Theatre of Louisville, a terrific ensemble play about male-female relationships in the 80's, was praised by *Newsweek* as "warm, vital, glowing . . . full of wise ironies and unsentimental hopes". The story concerns a weekend reunion of old college friends now in their early thirties. The occasion is the visit of Vanessa, the queen bee of the group, who is now the leader of a lesbian/feminist rock band. Vanessa arrives at the home of an old friend who is now a psychiatrist hand in hand with her naif-like lover, who also plays in the band. Also on hand are the psychiatrist's wife, a novelist suffering from writer's block; and his brother, who was once Vanessa's lover and who still loves her. In the course of the weekend, Vanessa reveals that she and her lover desperately want to have a child—and she tries to persuade her former male lover to father it, not understanding that he might have some feelings about the whole thing. *Time Magazine* heard "the unmistakable cry of an infant hit . . . Playwright Tolan's work radiates promise and achievement." (#25051)

(Royalty, $60-$40.)

PASTORALE
(LITTLE THEATRE—COMEDY)
By DEBORAH EISENBERG

3 men, 4 women—Interior
(plus 1 or 2 bit parts and 3 optional extras)

"Deborah Eisenberg is one of the freshest and funniest voices in some seasons."—Newsweek. Somewhere out in the country Melanie has rented a house and in the living room she, her friend Rachel who came for a weekend but forgets to leave, and their school friend Steve (all in their mid-20s) spend nearly a year meandering through a mental landscape including such concerns as phobias, friendship, work, sex, slovenliness and epistemology. Other people happen by: Steve's young girlfriend Celia, the virtuous and annoying Edie, a man who Melanie has picked up in a bar, and a couple who appear during an intense conversation and observe the sofa is on fire. The lives of the three friends inevitably proceed and eventually draw them, the better prepared perhaps by their months on the sofa, in separate directions. "The most original, funniest new comic voice to be heard in New York theater since Beth Henley's 'Crimes of the Heart.'"—N.Y. Times. "A very funny, stylish comedy."—The New Yorker. "Wacky charm and wayward wit."—New York Magazine. "Delightful."—N.Y. Post. "Uproarious . . . the play is a world unto itself, and it spins."—N.Y. Sunday Times. (#18016)

(Royalty, $50-$35.)

#W-26

SAMUEL FRENCH has:
AMERICA'S FAVORITE COMEDIES

ABSURD PERSON SINGULAR – ACCOMMODATIONS – ANGEL ON MY SHOULDER – BAREFOOT IN THE PARK – A BEDFULL OF FOREIGNERS – BEDROOM FARCE – BUTTERFLIES ARE FREE – CACTUS FLOWER – CALIFORNIA SUITE – CHAMPAGNE COMPLEX – CHAPTER TWO – CHARLIE'S AUNT – A COUPLA WHITE CHICKS – DON'T DRINK THE WATER – THE DREAM CRUST – FLING! – FOOLS – THE FOURPOSTER – THE GIN GAME – THE GINGERBREAD LADY – GOD'S FAVORITE THE GOOD DOCTOR – HERE LIES JEREMY TROY – I OUGHT TO BE IN PICTURES – THE IMPOSSIBLE YEARS – IN ONE BED . . . AND OUT THE OTHER – IT HAD TO BE YOU – KINDLING – THE LADY WHO CRIED FOX – LOVE, SEX AND THE I.R.S. – LOVERS AND OTHER STRANGERS – LUNCH HOUR – THE MARRIAGE-GO-ROUND

For descriptions of plays, consult our Basic Catalogue of Plays.